Cakes

by

Arlene Mueller

Illustrated by Craig Torlucci

© Copyright 1978
Nitty Gritty Productions
Concord, California

A Nitty Gritty Book*
Published by
Nitty Gritty Productions
P.O. Box 5457
Concord, California 94524

*Nitty Gritty Books - Trademark
Owned by Nitty Gritty Productions
Concord, California

ISBN 0-911954-48-1
Library of Congress Catalog Card Number: 78-52771

Table of Contents

A Cake For Every Occasion

When I was growing up in Minnesota an empty cake pan on the cupboard was a welcome sign that a cake would be in the oven soon. We'd all start guessing what kind when we saw the shape of the pan.

The 9 by 13 oblong pan might mean Banana Fudge or Oatmeal Cake. In Springtime it often would be warm Rhubarb Cake served with a pitcher of thick cream alongside. Layer pans came out less often but when they did, we'd be excited because they usually meant the famous Blitz Torte or Carrot Cake with its creamy cheese frosting. Bundt pans often announced a "kaffeeklatsch" and cupcake pans hinted of an upcoming picnic. When the springform pan and the antique-glass pedestal cake plate appeared we knew we'd soon be treated to the special Pedestal Cake.

Birthdays meant we could go to the cupboard and pull out the pans for our special-order cake. With a clatter I'd bring out the layer pans. Mom knew my choice - Chocolate Cake with Nut Custard Filling - no doubt about it!

The recipes for these favorite cakes, and many others, are included in the sections which follow along with hints for making better cakes of all kinds. I hope you, too, will discover that cake baking can be easy, fun and successful.

Basic Kinds of Cakes

"Butter" Cakes — Cakes using solid fat such as butter, margarine, vegetable shortening (Crisco, Spry, etc.) or lard.

Angel Food or Sponge Cakes — True sponge or angel food cakes contain no fat or baking powder. Stiffly beaten egg whites act as the levening agent.

Chiffon Cakes — Modified sponge cakes. The proportion of egg whites is lower, baking powder is used for levening, and oil is added for richness.

Conventional Method Cakes — "Butter" cakes made the traditional method of creaming sugar and shortening together until fluffy.

Quick Method Cakes — "Butter" cakes made the easy, one-bowl method. Creaming is eliminated. Always use vegetable shortening, not butter, margarine or lard. These cakes do not keep as well as other types of cakes.

Hints For Better Cakes

- Read the recipe carefully before starting to bake.
- Follow recipe and directions exactly.
- Never alter key ingredients - flour, sugar, shortening, eggs and liquid - since cakes are precisely balanced formulas.
- Measure carefully using standard measuring cups and spoons. All measurements are level.
- Don't double a recipe. To save time you can measure ingredients for more than one cake at a time, but keep everything separate. Mixing for each cake must be done individually.
- Be sure pans are the correct size called for in the recipe.
- All ingredients should be at room temperature (70° to 75°). Remove eggs, butter, milk, etc. from refrigerator at least one hour before using.
- Sift flour before measuring. Spoon flour into measuring cup heaping it up. Level off cup with the straight edge of a knife or spatula.
- Sift all dry ingredients, except sugar, together unless recipe indicates otherwise.
- After flour is added to cake mixture, batter must be disturbed as little as

3

possible to prevent the gluten (a protein substance found in wheat flour) from developing and resulting in a tough cake. "Butter" cake batter may be stirred gently for 1 to 2 minutes, but sponge cake batter should have only the minimum amount of folding necessary to blend ingredients.

- Always preheat oven. Reduce temperature 25 degrees for glass pans.
- Divide batter evenly between pans.
- Push batter to sides and corners of pan with spatula. Make a slight depression in center so cake will rise evenly.
- After cake begins to rise do not move it until it is fully risen and set; then only if necessary.
- Do not crowd the oven. Place cakes in the oven in this manner:

single layer - Bake on rack in center of oven.

two layers - Bake on rack in center of oven. Do not let pans touch sides of oven or each other.

three layers - Bake on 2 racks placed so they divide oven in thirds. Stagger pans so one is not directly over another.

●Test for doneness by inserting a toothpick into cake near center. If it comes out clean, cake is done. Or press lightly in center with finger - cake will spring back when completely baked.

●Let cake cool at least 5 to 10 minutes (on cake racks) before attempting to remove from pan. Do not force. Loosen edges with spatula. If cake sticks, turn pan on each side successively and hold in each position long enough for cake to loosen itself by its own weight.

●To remove cake from pan place inverted cake rack over top of pan. Then turn cake and rack over; remove pan. Place another inverted rack over bottom of cake. Turn cake and rack over and cake will be right side up.

●Dust cake plate with a little powdered sugar before placing cake on it. This allows the cake to be easily moved if it needs centering.

●In an emergency, if recipe calls for cake flour, it is possible to achieve a successful cake by decreasing the amount of all-purpose flour by 2 tablespoons per cup (ie: 1 cup, use 7/8 cup) or, for each cup of cake flour needed measure 2 tablespoons cornstarch into a 1 cup measure and fill cup with flour. Sift together several times.

Basic Strokes

Because proper mixing techniques are so important to the success of a cake, understanding the basic strokes is an essential part of the careful preparation required in cake baking.

Cream - Combining fat and sugar, either by hand with the back of a wooden spoon in a back and forth motion pressing the mixture between the back of the spoon and the side of the bowl, or with an electric mixer on lowest speed. Cream only until batter is light colored, smooth and creamy. If it looks curdled it is overworked causing the oil in the butter to separate resulting in a coarsely grained cake.

Stir - Using a wooden spoon, begin at the center of mixing bowl moving in a circular motion and widening the circle as ingredients become blended. An electric mixer set on lowest speed may be used for stirring.

Beat - Using free, vigorous, lifting motions, going from top to bottom, trapping in as much air as possible. Beating with an electric mixer is done on medium speed.

Whip - Whipping is beating rapidly. Some chefs prefer using a whisk and copper bowl for greater volume, but I have always obtained excellent results using an electric beater on high speed. Use the one you prefer.

Fold - To blend ingredients (usually egg whites and batter) thoroughly with a rubber scraper, going from top to bottom, across and over top and down again, turning bowl a quarter turn after each stroke, without losing any of the air you have carefully incorporated into egg whites, etc.

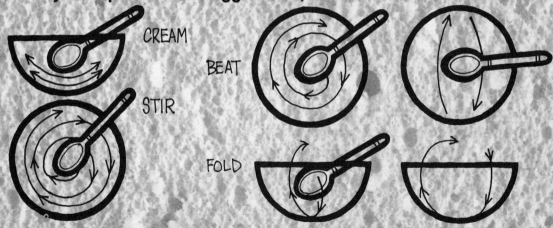

CREAM

STIR

BEAT

FOLD

Topping Them Off

The words "icing" and "frosting" are used interchangeably. The terms originated from the idea of a dull-white covering - like ice or frost - for a cake.

- Place hot cake on rack to allow for air circulation until ready to remove it from pan. Return cake to rack until ready to frost. Uncooked frosting is best spread on a slightly warm cake; cooked frosting is best on a cooled cake.
- If necessary trim cake to make it smooth and symmetrical.
- Brush away all coarse crumbs.
- Select a cake plate or tray that is flat and 2 or 3 inches larger in diameter than the cake. Cut 4 pieces of waxed paper full width by 5 inches long. Fold in half lengthwise. Lay strips, folded edge toward center, on the outer edges of plate before cake is placed there. Position cake on top of strips. Frost cake. When hardening begins, gently remove papers one at a time.
- To frost, place first cake layer in center of plate, bottom side up. Spread frosting on top. Let set slightly. Place top layer right side up on first layer, with bottoms together.
- If cake begins to slip, skewer layers together with toothpicks or small metal skewers until frosting sets.

- Frost sides of cake first, bringing frosting from bottom up over top.
- Frost top last, swirling the frosting as you spread.
- A textured surface is usually preferred to a smooth, glossy one unless a design is to be applied.
- If a glossy surface is desired, dip spatula frequently into hot water while frosting cake.
- Be sure to apply nuts, candies, etc., before icing hardens.

PLATE UNDERNEATH

PLACE CAKE ON TOP & FROST

REMOVE PAPERS

Round Cakes & Cupcakes

11

LaRUE'S GOLDEN LAYER CAKE

2-1/4 cups sifted cake flour
3 tsp. baking powder
1 tsp. salt
1-1/3 cups sugar
1/4 cup Crisco or Spry
1/4 cup butter, softened
1 cup milk
1 tsp. vanilla extract
2 large eggs
Pineapple Filling, page 13
Seven Minute Frosting, page 14

12

Sift and measure flour. Sift again with other dry ingredients into mixing bowl. Add vanilla to milk. Add shortening and butter and two-thirds of milk to dry ingredients. Stir on slow mixer speed for 3 minutes, scraping sides of bowl often. Add remaining milk and unbeaten eggs. Continue beating on medium speed for 2 to 3 minutes. Batter will be thin enough to pour easily. Pour into 2 greased and floured 9-inch layer pans. Bake at 350°F. for 30 minutes or until done. May be baked in a 9 by 13-inch pan 30 to 35 minutes. Frost either version with Seven Minute Frosting. Fill layer cake with Pineapple Filling.

PINEAPPLE FILLING

2 tbs. cornstarch
1/2 cup sugar
1 cup crushed pineapple, undrained
1 tbs. lemon juice

Mix cornstarch with sugar. Add pineapple and juice and cook slowly until thick and clear. Cool before spreading on bottom layer. Save one-half cup of pineapple filling for decorating cake top.

SEVEN MINUTE FROSTING

2 egg whites, unbeaten
1-1/2 cups sugar
2 tsp. light corn syrup
dash salt
1/3 cup water
1 tsp. vanilla extract

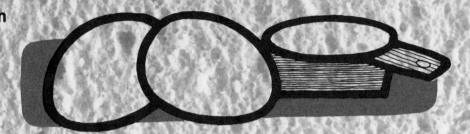

14

Combine egg whites, sugar, corn syrup, salt and water in top of double boiler. Beat about 1 minute or until thoroughly mixed. Cook over rapidly boiling water, beating constantly 7 minutes or until frosting will stand up in stiff peaks. Remove from boiling water. Add vanilla and beat 1 additional minute or until thick enough to spread. Makes enough for 9-inch layer cake. One-half of this recipe is adequate for a 9 by 13-inch.

BLITZ TORTE

In German it means "lightning cake" and it goes together in a flash.

1/2 cup butter	1 cup sifted cake flour
1 cup sugar	2 tsp. baking powder
3 eggs, separated	1/4 tsp. salt
5 tbs. milk	1/2 cup sugar
1 tsp. vanilla or almond extract	1/2 cup finely chopped walnuts or almonds

Cream butter and 1/2 cup sugar. Add egg yolks separately, beating after each addition. Add milk and vanilla. Sift dry ingredients together and stir into creamed mixture. Spread batter in 2 greased and floured 9-inch layer pans. Beat egg whites with remaining 1/2 cup sugar. Spread on top of batter. Sprinkle nuts on top. Bake 30 to 35 minutes at 350°F. Cool and place layers together with a fresh fruit mixture between, or cut in single-layer wedges and spoon fruit or other topping over individual pieces.

ARLENE'S BIRTHDAY CAKE

Beaten egg whites create a smooth icing that melts in your mouth.

1/4 cup Crisco or Spry
1/4 cup butter, softened
1-1/4 cups sugar
2 eggs
2 sq. (1 oz. ea.) unsweetened chocolate, melted
2 cups sifted cake flour
1/2 tsp. salt
1 tsp. baking soda
1 cup buttermilk
Custard Filling, page 17
Chocolate Fluff, page 18

Cream shortening and butter with sugar. Beat in eggs one at a time. Add melted chocolate. Sift dry ingredients together. Add to creamed mixture, alternately with milk, beginning and ending with flour. Beat briefly after each

addition, scraping down sides of bowl. Pour into two greased and floured 9-inch layer pans and bake at 350°F. for 30 minutes or until done. When cool, spread with Custard Filling and frost with Chocolate Fluff.

CUSTARD FILLING

1 cup warm milk
2 egg yolks, beaten
1/4 cup sugar
1 tbs. flour

dash salt
1 tsp. vanilla extract
1/3 cup chopped walnuts

Warm milk in small saucepan. In separate saucepan beat egg yolks. Gradually stir in sugar, flour and salt, which have been mixed together. Pour half of milk into sugar mixture, stirring until well mixed. Add remaining milk, stirring until smooth. Cook over medium heat, stirring constantly, until thick. Remove from heat. Cool. Stir in vanilla and nuts when thoroughly cooled.

CHOCOLATE FLUFF

3/4 cup powdered sugar
1/4 tsp. salt
4 tbs. butter, soft but not melted
1 tsp. vanilla extract
2 sq. (1 oz. ea.) unsweetened chocolate, melted
2 egg whites, stiffly beaten
3/4 cup powdered sugar

Cream sugar, salt and butter with spoon until fluffy. Add vanilla and melted chocolate. In separate bowl, beat egg whites until stiff but not dry. Gently fold in powdered sugar, 2 tablespoonfuls at a time. Fold several tablespoonfuls egg whites into chocolate mixture. Gradually and gently fold in remaining whites until white streams disappear. Frosting will be soft, but will later set slightly.

Note - For a special higher cake, bake in 3, 8 or 9-inch layer pans and increase filling recipe by one-half.

PINEAPPLE UPSIDE DOWN SKILLET CAKE

Use apricots for a delicious change. The topping is brown sugar rich.

2/3 cup butter
1 cup brown sugar
1 can (20 ozs.) pineapple rings
3 eggs, separated
3/4 cup white sugar

5 tbs. juice from pineapple
1 cup sifted flour
1 tsp. baking powder
pinch salt
cherries and nuts or coconut

Melt butter and brown sugar in a 10 to 12-inch skillet (mine is cast iron) over low heat. Arrange pineapple rings in skillet and let simmer. Meanwhile beat egg yolks until light and fluffy. Add sugar and fruit juice. Sift flour with baking powder and salt. Fold into sugar/egg mixture. Beat egg whites until stiff, but not dry. Fold into batter. Arrange cherries and nuts or coconut in a decorative way around pineapple before pouring cake batter over fruit. Bake at 350°F. 40 to 45 minutes or until toothpick inserted into center of cake comes out clean. Immediately cover skillet with cake plate. Invert plate and cake. Leave pan over cake for a few minutes allowing caramelized syrup to run down over cake.

CREAM 'N CARROT CAKE

Pineapple bits set this carrot cake apart from others.

2 cups sifted flour
2 tsp. baking powder
1-1/2 tsp. baking soda
1 tsp. salt
2 tsp. cinnamon
2 cups sugar
1-1/2 cups Wesson oil
4 eggs
2 cups finely grated carrots
1 can (13 ozs.) crushed pineapple, <u>well drained</u>
1 cup walnuts, chopped
Cream Cheese Frosting, page 21

Sift flour and measure. Sift a second time with baking powder, soda, salt, cinnamon and sugar. Add oil and eggs and blend well. Reserve 2 tablespoons

pineapple for frosting. Add remaining pineapple and carrots to cake batter stirring until thoroughly mixed. Fold in walnuts. Bake in 3, 9-inch greased and floured layer pans for 30 minutes at 350°F. Frost when slightly cool.

CREAM CHEESE FROSTING

1 cube (1/2 cup) butter
1 package (8 ozs.) cream cheese
1 tsp. vanilla extract
1 box (1 lb.) powdered sugar
2 tbs. well-drained crushed pineapple

Cream softened butter with cream cheese until smooth and well blended. Add vanilla. Gradually add powdered sugar, stirring until totally smooth. Stir in pineapple. This recipe makes a generous amount. You will use it for the filling as well as for the top and sides of the cake.

APPLESAUCE CUPCAKES

1-1/2 cups sifted cake flour
1-1/3 cups sugar
1 cup applesauce
2/3 cup Crisco
1 tsp. salt
3-1/2 tsp. baking powder
3 eggs
1 tbs. grated orange rind
Creamy Icing, page 33

22

Combine flour, sugar, 1/2 cup applesauce, Crisco and salt in bowl. Beat vigorously by hand or mixer for 2 minutes. Stir in baking powder. (Batter will be very thick.) Add remaining 1/2 cup applesauce, eggs and orange rind. Beat for 2 additional minutes. Fill cupcake pans 1/2 full with batter. Bake at 400°F. 10 to 12 minutes. Frost with Creamy Icing. Makes about 1-1/2 dozen large cupcakes.

PRUNE TEATIME CAKES

1 cup <u>uncooked</u> pitted prunes
1 cup boiling water
2 cups sifted flour
1-1/2 cups sugar
1 tsp. salt

1-1/4 tsp. baking soda
1 tsp. <u>each</u> cinnamon, nutmeg, cloves
1/2 cup oil
3 eggs, unbeaten
1 cup chopped nuts

Cut prunes into small pieces. Pour boiling water over prunes. Let stand 2 hours. Sift dry ingredients together into large bowl. Add prune mixture, oil, eggs and nuts. Blend thoroughly for about 1 minute. Then beat 2 minutes on medium speed of mixer or 300 strokes by hand. Bake in paper-lined muffin pans 20 to 25 minutes at 350°F. Makes 12 cupcakes. Frost with Creamy Icing, page 33, or sprinkle before baking with Streusel Topping. This recipe adapts well to a 9 by 13 cake (bake 45 to 50 minutes at 350°F.) or two 9-inch layers (bake 35 to 40 minutes at 350°F.).

STREUSEL TOPPING - Mix 1/2 cup brown or white sugar, 2 tablespoons flour and 2 tablespoons soft butter until crumbly. Sprinkle on top of batter before baking. Serve warm.

23

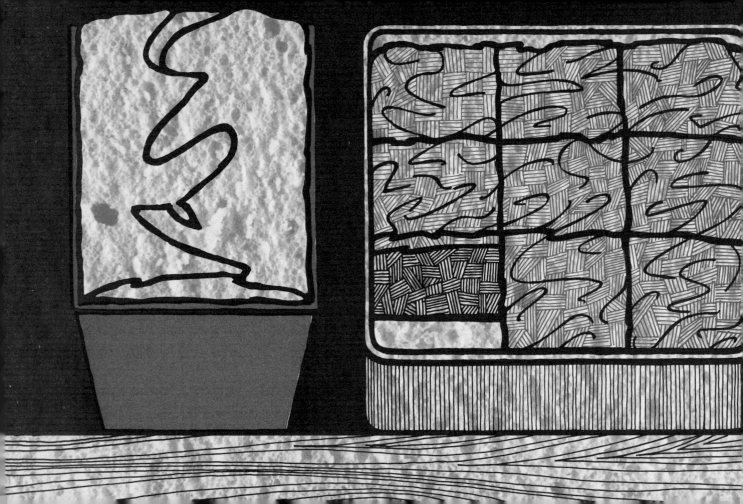

Square Cakes & Loaf Cakes

Cafe Chocolate	35
Caramel Frosting	31
Cranberry Cake	30
Creamy Icing	33
Fluffy Lemon Sauce	29
Fresh Apple Cake	32
Fresh Fruit Meringue Cake	26
Gold Cake	31
Hot Butter Sauce	30
Meringue	27
Old-Time Gingerbread	28
Sicilian Strega Cake	36
Sour Cream Loaf	35
White Fruit Cake	34

FRESH FRUIT MERINGUE CAKE

Any fresh fruit is delicious but a combination of fresh plums and nectarines is a summertime favorite. Canned pineapple or frozen berries are also good.

1 cup plus 1 tbs. sifted cake flour
1/2 cup sugar
1-1/2 tsp. baking powder
1/2 tsp. salt
1/4 cup oil
2 egg yolks, unbeaten

1/3 cup cold water
1 tsp. vanilla extract
1 tbs. grated lemon rind
4 egg whites
1/2 tsp. cream of tartar
1/4 cup sugar

26

Sift flour, sugar, baking powder and salt together. Make a well and add oil, egg yolks, water, vanilla and lemon rind. Beat until smooth. Combine egg whites and cream of tartar in separate bowl. Whip until foamy. Add the 1/4 cup sugar, 1 tablespoon at a time, beating until stiff peaks form. Gently fold egg yolk mixture into beaten whites just until blended. Pour batter into an 8 by 8-inch, waxed paper-lined pan. Bake at 350°F. 40 to 45 minutes. Remove from pan. Cool and place on baking sheet. Prepare meringue.

MERINGUE

2 egg whites
1/4 tsp. salt
1/2 tsp. cream of tartar
1/2 cup sugar
sliced fresh fruit, canned crushed pineapple or frozen berries

Beat egg whites, salt and cream of tartar until foamy. Add sugar, 1 tablespoon at a time. Continue beating 10 to 15 minutes, or until meringue forms stiff peaks. Spread over cake. Place cake in 425°F. oven 4 to 5 minutes - just long enough to brown peaks. Cut into squares and spoon fruit over the top of each serving.

OLD-TIME GINGERBREAD

The perfect dessert after a supper of hearty soup. Serve with hot spiced tea.

1/2 cup butter
1/2 cup strong, hot coffee
1-1/2 cups flour
1 tsp. ginger

2 eggs, unbeaten
1/2 cup sugar
1/2 cup Brer Rabbit molasses
2 tsp. baking powder

Dissolve butter in hot coffee. Sift flour and ginger together. Beat eggs. Add sugar and molasses. Stir in warm coffee mixture. Mix in flour. Add baking powder last. Pour batter into greased and floured 8 by 8-inch pan. Bake 25 minutes at 350°F. Cut into squares while warm. Serve with sweetened whipped cream, or spread apricot jam on top of warm cake, or pass a bowl of chilled applesauce with cake. Or, go really special with Fluffy Lemon Sauce, page 29. To make more like a cake-dessert, frost <u>while hot</u> with a mixture of 1 cup powdered sugar and 4 tablespoons cream, flavored with vanilla and lemon rind.

Variation - Add 1/2 teaspoon <u>each</u> cinnamon, allspice and cloves along with the ginger for a spicier gingerbread.

FLUFFY LEMON SAUCE

2/3 cup sugar
2 tbs. cornstarch
1/4 tsp. salt
1/3 cup lemon juice
1 cup water
1 tsp. grated lemon rind
1 cup heavy cream, whipped

Combine sugar, cornstarch, and salt in saucepan. Gradually add lemon juice and water. Cook over medium heat, stirring constantly, until mixture thickens and is clear. Boil 1 minute. Remove from heat and cool, stirring occasionally. Stir in rind. Fold in whipped cream. Makes about 2-1/2 cups.

CRANBERRY CAKE

This "saucy" cake is made without eggs.

1 cup sugar　　　　　　　1 tsp. salt
3 tbs. butter　　　　　　　1 cup milk
2 cups sifted flour　　　　2 cups raw cranberries, halved
2 tsp. baking powder

Cream sugar and butter. Sift dry ingredients together. Add to creamed mixture alternately with milk. Fold cranberries in last. Pour batter into greased 8 by 8-inch pan. Bake at 350°F. 1 hour or until cake tests done. Cut into squares.

HOT BUTTER SAUCE

1/2 cup butter　　　　　　1/2 cup cream
1 cup sugar　　　　　　　1 tsp. vanilla extract

Boil ingredients together 1 minute. Serve hot sauce over cake squares.

GOLD CAKE

My husband's first choice for his birthday.

1 cup butter
2 cups sugar
8 egg yolks, well beaten
1 cup water
3 cups sifted cake flour

3 tsp. baking powder
1 tbs. lemon juice
or 1 tsp. vanilla extract
Caramel Frosting

Cream butter, sugar and well beaten egg yolks. Add water and flour, which has been sifted with baking powder. Stir until smooth. Add lemon juice. Pour into 1 greased and lightly floured 5 by 9-inch loaf pan (or 2, 4 by 8-inch loaf pans). Bake at 350°F. 1 hour or until cake tests done. Frost top and sides with Caramel Frosting or Penuche Frosting, page 41.

CARAMEL FROSTING - Cook 1/2 cup heavy cream, 2 cups brown sugar and 1 tablespoon butter until thick. Remove from heat and add 1 teaspoon vanilla extract. Beat until spreading consistency. Add more cream if too thick.

FRESH APPLE CAKE

Apples, walnuts, cinnamon and lemon blend into a memorable dessert.

2 cups cubed raw, unpeeled apples
1 egg, unbeaten
1 cup sugar
1/4 cup oil
1 cup chopped walnuts
1/4 tsp. vanilla extract

1 tsp. cinnamon
1 cup sifted flour
1 tsp. baking soda
1/4 tsp. salt
1 tbs. lemon rind
Creamy Icing, page 33

Combine apples and egg in bowl. Mix well. Stir in sugar and oil until well mixed. Add walnuts, vanilla and cinnamon. Sift dry ingredients together and stir into mixture. Add rind last. Pour batter into greased 4 by 8-inch loaf pan. Bake 40 minutes at 350°F. Frost with Creamy Icing.

CREAMY ICING

Everyone loves this unusual icing.

2-1/3 cups sifted powdered sugar
1/4 tsp. salt
1 egg
2 tbs. water
1/4 cup sugar
1/2 cup Crisco (don't substitute butter or margarine)
1 tsp. vanilla extract

Mix powdered sugar, salt and egg. Boil water and sugar together for 1 minute. Blend with egg mixture. Add Crisco and vanilla. Beat until creamy.

WHITE FRUIT CAKE

For a white Christmas at your house, try our white fruit cake.

1 lb. dates, pitted and reclosed
1 lb. walnut halves
1 lb. shelled <u>whole</u> brazil nuts
1 jar (9 oz.) green cherries, drained
1 jar (9 oz.) red cherries, drained
1-1/2 cups sifted flour
1 tsp. baking powder
1-1/2 cups sugar
4 eggs, beaten

34

Coat dates, nuts and cherries with 1/2 cup flour. Sift remaining flour with baking powder. Mix sugar and eggs. Add flour gradually, stirring until mixed. Fold in nuts and fruit. Line 2, 4 by 8-inch loaf pans with 2 sheets of buttered waxed paper. Bake at 325°F. for 1 hour. Makes 2 loaves.

SOUR CREAM LOAF

Serve this tangy vanilla cake with Café Chocolate for a late evening snack.

1 cup sugar
2 tbs. butter
3 eggs, separated
1 tsp. vanilla extract
2 cups sifted flour

2 tsp. baking powder
1 cup sour cream
1/2 cup cold water
1/2 tsp. salt

Cream sugar and butter. Beat in egg yolks and vanilla. Sift flour and baking powder together. Add to mixture in thirds, alternating with sour cream and water. Beat egg whites and salt until stiff, but not dry. Fold into batter. Pour batter into greased 9 by 5-inch loaf pan. Bake at 375°F. 40 minutes. Frost with Orange Butter Frosting, page 57, your favorite frosting, or serve with berries.

CAFE CHOCOLATE: Make a pot of coffee. Prepare an equal amount of hot cocoa using milk. Combine the two. Pour into serving cups and top with whipped cream.

SICILIAN STREGA CAKE

This was my birthday cake in Florence, Italy - purchased right near the Duomo. There is no substitute for Strega, the golden liqueur.

1 (4 by 8-in.) Buttermilk Pound Cake, page 71, or Sara Lee Pound Cake
1 lb. ricotta cheese
3 oz. well drained maraschino cherries, finely chopped
3 ozs. semisweet chocolate, finely chopped
3 tbs. Strega
9 ozs. semisweet chocolate, broken in pieces
1/3 cup strong black coffee
1/2 lb. sweet unsalted butter

Freeze cake briefly so it will be easier to slice. Slice into 6 or 7 horizontal layers. Set all but the bottom one aside. Mix cheese, cherries, chopped chocolate and Strega together. Spread some of mixture on bottom layer, carefully covering cake evenly and including corners. Continue adding layers and spreading cheese mixture between them. Top layer of cake will be without mixture. Be certain cake has not become lop-sided. If necessary, stick toothpicks through top of cake to hold firmly together. Using a spatula, smooth sides of cake and fill in any spots lacking filling. At this point you may cover the cake with foil and refrigerate overnight or a few hours, or you may frost it.

Melt broken pieces of chocolate in a bowl over hot water. Add coffee and stir until smooth. Off the heat add butter, 1 tablespoon at a time, stirring well after each addition until completely smooth. This will take about 30 minutes. When all butter is stirred in, the mixture will be too thin to use for icing cake. Set in refrigerator to thicken slightly. <u>Watch carefully so it does not become hard.</u> When mixture is spreadable, frost sides of cake first and top last. The frosting is extra thick for the size of the cake, but that is what is so special. Create waves on top and use a frosting "comb" or utensil to make straight lines on sides. Frosting will harden and form a chocolate shell around the moist cake layers. Make the slices small. Serve with strong coffee.

Oblong Cakes

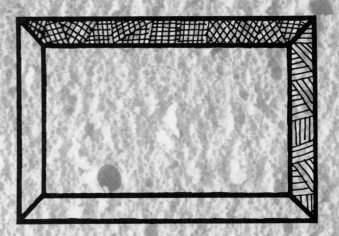

39

BANANA NUT CAKE

1/2 cup Crisco (or part butter)
1 cup sugar
2 eggs, separated
1 tsp. vanilla extract
1 cup mashed <u>ripe</u> bananas
1 tsp. baking soda

3/4 tsp. baking powder
dash salt
2 cups sifted cake flour
3/4 cup buttermilk
1 cup chopped nuts

40

Cream Crisco and sugar. Add egg yolks and vanilla. Beat well. Add bananas Sift dry ingredients together and add to creamed mixture alternately with milk. Add nuts. Beat egg whites until stiff but not dry. Fold into batter. Spread batter in greased and floured 9 by 13-inch pan. Bake at 350°F. 40 minutes (30 minutes if a layer cake is desired). Frost with Penuche Frosting, page 41, or Sea Foam Frosting, page 42, or Real Fudge Frosting, page 43.

PENUCHE FROSTING

1/2 cup butter
1 cup firmly packed brown sugar
1/4 cup milk
2 cups powdered sugar, <u>well sifted</u>

Melt butter in small saucepan. Stir in brown sugar and bring mixture to a boil. Reduce heat and simmer for 2 minutes, stirring constantly. Add milk and bring mixture to a boil, stirring constantly. Remove from heat and let mixture cool. Gradually stir in powdered sugar and beat until consistency for spreading.

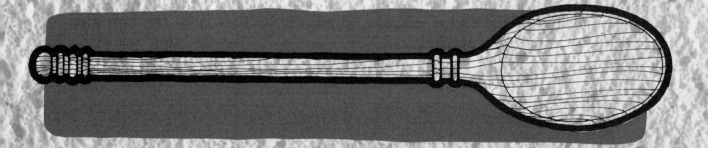

SEA FOAM FROSTING

2 egg whites, unbeaten
1-1/2 cups brown sugar
dash salt
1/3 cup water
1 tsp. vanilla extract

42

Combine egg whites, sugar, salt and water in top of double boiler. Beat with rotary egg beater or electric beater about 1 minute or until thoroughly mixed. Cook over rapidly boiling water, beating constantly for 7 minutes, or until frosting will stand up in stiff peaks. Occasionally stir frosting from bottom of pan. Remove from boiling water. Add vanilla and beat 1 minute or until thick enough to spread. This recipe makes enough frosting to cover top and sides of layer cake or 2 dozen cupcakes.

REAL FUDGE FROSTING

Old-fashioned candy fudge topping.

1-1/2 cups sugar	2 tbs. cocoa
3/4 cup milk	1 tsp. vanilla extract
1/4 tsp. salt	1 tsp. butter

Mix sugar, milk, cocoa and salt together. Stir well. Cook slowly over medium heat until mixture comes to a boil. Continue boiling until soft ball stage is reached. When mixture begins to thicken and drips slowly from spoon it is approaching soft ball stage. This may take 15 minutes. (Test by dripping several drops of mixture into cup of cold water. It will form a soft ball with fingertips when ready.) Remove mixture from heat. Add butter and vanilla, stirring until well mixed. Beat with spoon until spreading consistency. This will take about 15 minutes. You may hasten the thickening by placing pan in pan of ice cubes and water. This procedure requires careful watching as frosting may thicken too quickly and not spread easily.

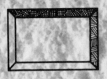

DEVIL'S FOOD MAYONNAISE CAKE

The eggs and shortening for this cake are already in the mayonnaise. Be sure to use real mayonnaise, not salad dressing.

2 cups sifted flour
1/2 tsp. salt
1-1/2 tsp. baking soda
5 tbs. cocoa
1 cup mayonnaise

1 cup sugar
3/4 cup water
2 tsp. vanilla extract
Chip Frosting

44

Sift flour, salt, soda and cocoa together. Whip mayonnaise, sugar, water and vanilla until mixed thoroughly. Add dry ingredients slowly. Beat at medium mixer speed or by hand for 2 minutes. Pour into greased and floured 9 by 13-inch pan. Bake at 350°F. for 20 to 25 minutes or until toothpick comes out clean.

CHIP FROSTING - Boil 1-1/2 cups sugar, 6 tablespoons butter and 7 tablespoons milk for 1 minute. Remove from heat. Add 1/2 cup semisweet chocolate chips. Beat until thick. Spread on top and sides of cake.

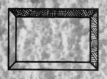

SPICE RAISIN CAKE

This is my Dad's usual birthday choice. For a real treat he'd ask for "a little cake with my frosting," and we'd double the recipe for Fudge Frosting.

1 cup brown sugar
1/2 cup butter
1 egg, beaten
dash salt
2 cups sifted flour
1 tsp. baking powder

1 tsp. baking soda
1 tsp. <u>each</u> cloves, cinnamon, nutmeg and ginger
1 cup milk or sour milk
1 cup chopped raisins
Real Fudge Frosting, page 43

45

Cream brown sugar and butter thoroughly. Add beaten egg. Sift dry ingredients together and add alternately with milk stirring gently after each addition. Add raisins. Bake in greased and lightly floured 9 by 13-inch pan for 30 to 40 minutes at 350°F. Frost with Fudge Frosting.

CALIFORNIA PEACH(OR APRICOT) CAKE

Test carefully - this is a moist cake and you could easily be fooled as to doneness.

1 cup raisins
1 cup Crisco
1-1/2 cups sugar
2 eggs
2 cups fresh, peeled, mashed peaches or
    unpeeled mashed apricots

2 cups sifted flour
1 tsp. <u>each</u> allspice, cloves,
    cinnamon
2 tsp. baking soda
2 tsp. cocoa

Partially cook raisins, or plump them in hot water for 30 minutes. Drain and dry on paper towels. Cream shortening, sugar and eggs. Heat mashed peaches. Add with natural juice to creamed mixture. Dredge raisins in a small amount of flour. Sift dry ingredients together and blend into peach mixture. Add raisins. Spread batter in greased and floured 9 by 13-inch pan. Bake 30 to 40 minutes at 350°F. Serve plain or with whipped cream. For a second day perk-up, spread with Lazy Daisy Frosting, page 47, and broil as directed. Serve warm.

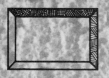

LAZY DAISY FROSTING

3 tbs. melted butter
5 tbs. brown sugar
2 tbs. cream or evaporated milk
1/2 cup coconut
1/4 cup chopped walnuts, optional

Thoroughly mix ingredients together in a bowl. Spread evenly on hot or leftover cake, making sure corners are well frosted. Place under broil until lightly browned and bubbly. Watch carefully. Double recipe for 9 by 13-inch cake.

Variation - One cup nuts may be used in place of coconut/nut combination.

CINNAMON-TOPPED RHUBARB CAKE

1/2 cup Crisco
1-1/2 cups sugar
1/2 tsp. salt
1 egg
1 tsp. baking soda
1 cup buttermilk
2 cups plus 1 tbs. sifted flour
3 cups finely cut rhubarb
1/3 cup sugar
1/3 cup nuts
1 tsp. cinnamon

48

Cream shortening and sugar. Add salt and beat in egg. Mix soda and milk together. Add alternately with flour, beginning and ending with flour. Fold in rhubarb. Pour into greased and floured 9 by 13-inch pan. Mix sugar, nuts and cinnamon together and sprinkle over cake batter. Bake 45 minutes at 350°F.

LUSANDRA'S MANDARIN ORANGE CAKE

2 cups sifted flour
2 cups sugar
1/2 tsp. salt
2 tsp. baking soda
2 eggs, unbeaten
2 tsp. vanilla extract
2 cans (11 ozs. ea.) mandarin oranges, <u>well-drained</u>
1 cup finely chopped nuts

Sift dry ingredients together. Add remaining ingredients and beat for 3 minutes with mixer at medium speed. Pour into greased and floured 9 by 13-inch pan. Bake at 350°F. for 30 minutes or until cake tests done. Serve with whipped cream or Special Topping.

SPECIAL TOPPING - Bring 2 cups brown sugar, 4 tablespoons softened butter and 6 tablespoons milk to a boil. Prick holes in cake top with toothpick or fork tines. Pour Special Topping over hot cake.

OATMEAL CAKE — CRUNCHY FROSTING

Also good with Real Fudge Frosting, page 43, or Lemon Icing, page 57.

1 cup uncooked quick oats
1-1/2 cups boiling water
1 cup white sugar
1 cup brown sugar

1/4 cup butter
1/4 cup Crisco or Spry
2 eggs, unbeaten
1 tsp. vanilla extract

1-1/2 cups sifted flour
1 tsp. cinnamon
1 tsp. baking soda
3/4 tsp. salt

50

Measure oats into mixing bowl. Add boiling water, stir and cool. Cream sugar, butter and shortening. Add eggs and vanilla. Beat well. Sift dry ingredients together. Add oatmeal mixture and sifted dry ingredients alternately to creamed mixture. Pour batter into greased and floured 9 by 13-inch pan. Bake 30 to 40 minutes at 350°F. Have Crunchy Frosting mixed. Spread over hot cake and place under broiler for a few minutes to brown. Watch carefully.

CRUNCHY FROSTING - Combine 6 tablespoons melted butter, 1/4 cup cream or evaporated milk, 1/2 teaspoon vanilla, 2/3 cup brown sugar and 1 cup coconut.

LEMON BITES

A very special moist cake chosen by my friend Anne for her wedding.

7 tbs. sweet unsalted butter
3/4 cup sugar
2 eggs
1/2 cup warm milk
1-1/2 cups sifted flour

1-1/2 tsp. baking powder
1/4 tsp. salt
3 tbs. grated lemon rind
1/2 cup fresh lemon juice
1/2 cup powdered sugar

Cream butter and sugar, Beat eggs until creamy. Add to creamed mixtures. Sift dry ingredients together. Using a wooden spoon stir milk into creamed mixture. Blend in dry ingredients. Fold in lemon rind. Pour batter into a buttered 9 by 13-inch pan or a jelly roll pan. Bake at 350°F. 25 minutes. Mix lemon juice and powdered sugar. Pour mixture over hot cake to form glaze. Return to oven for a minute or two until top becomes textured. Cut pieces according to use - bar size for the cookie plate or larger size as a base for fruit sauce or flavored whipped cream. This cake freezes exceptionally well. Cut into pieces and place between layers of waxed paper. Wrap well in foil and freeze.

Bundt Cakes

53

CHOCOLATE-CHERRY CAKE

A heavy cake that needs no topping and stays moist for days. I always use pie filling which has no preservatives.

2 cups sifted flour
3/4 cup sugar
3/4 cup vegetable oil
2 eggs, unbeaten
2 tsp. vanilla extract
1 tsp. baking soda

1 tsp. cinnamon
1/8 tsp. salt
1 can (21 ozs.) cherry pie filling
1 pkg. (6 ozs.) semisweet chocolate morsels
1 cup chopped nuts

Preheat oven to 350°F. Combine flour, sugar, oil, eggs, vanilla, soda, cinnamon and salt in large bowl. Mix well. Stir in pie filling, chocolate morsels and nuts. Pour into greased and floured 10-cup bundt pan. Bake at 350°F. 1 hour, or until done. Cool 10 minutes. Remove from pan and sprinkle with powdered sugar.

54

ORANGE GROVE CAKE

Nutty Topping
3/4 cup butter
1 cup sugar
3 tbs. grated orange rind
1 tsp. vanilla
3 eggs, unbeaten
1/2 cup orange marmalade

3 cups sifted all-purpose flour
1 tsp. salt
1 tsp. <u>each</u> baking powder and soda
1/2 cup <u>each</u> orange juice and
evaporated milk
1 cup walnuts, chopped

55

Prepare Nutty Topping. Butter a 10-cup bundt pan well. Pat topping on bottom and sides (not on the center tube) of the pan. Cream butter and sugar. Mix in orange rind and vanilla. Add eggs and beat well. Stir in marmalade. Sift dry ingredients together. Add to creamed mixture alternately with orange juice and milk. Fold in nuts. Turn batter into prepared pan. Bake at 350°F. about 70 minutes. Cool before removing from pan.

NUTTY TOPPING - Mix 1/2 cup sugar, 1/2 cup butter, 1/2 cup dry bread crumbs and 1/2 cup finely chopped walnuts or almonds together until crumbly.

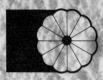

KATIE'S POPPY SEED CAKE

Let all ingredients stand at room temperature 2 to 3 hours before using.

1/3 cup poppy seed
1 cup buttermilk
3/4 cup sugar
1 cup powdered sugar
1 cup butter
4 eggs, separated
1 tsp. vanilla extract
1 tsp. almond extract

2-1/2 cups sifted flour
1 tsp. baking powder
1 tsp. baking soda
dash salt
3 tbs. sugar
1 tbs. <u>each</u> cinnamon and nutmeg
Butter Rum Icing, page 57

56

Soak poppy seed in buttermilk 15 minutes. Sift sugars together. Cream butter and sugars. Add unbeaten egg yolks one at a time, beating until smooth after each addition. Add vanilla and almond extract. Sift flour and dry ingredients together 3 times. Add flour and milk to creamed mixture in 3 additions, starting and ending with flour. Beat egg whites until stiff but not dry. Fold into batter. Pour half of batter into well-buttered, 10-cup bundt pan.

Sprinkle with sugar, cinnamon and nutmeg. Add remaining batter. Bake at 350°F. 45 minutes or until done. Let cake stand 15 minutes before removing from pan. It is delicious without any topping, but if you wish, add a lemon glaze or frost with Butter Rum Icing, page 57, and sprinkle poppy seed on top.

BUTTER RUM ICING

3 tbs. soft butter
2 cups sifted powdered sugar

1/4 tsp. salt
3 tbs. rum

Beat butter until fluffy in small bowl. Add sifted sugar gradually. Blend until creamy. Stir until perfectly smooth. If too thick, add more rum. If too thin, add more sugar. For Orange or Lemon Icing: Substitute orange or lemon juice for rum. Add 1 tablespoon finely grated orange or lemon rind. For Vanilla or Almond Icing: Substitute cream for rum. Add 1 teaspoon vanilla or almond extract.

HUNGARIAN CINNAMON KUCHEN

FILLING

3/4 cup dark brown sugar
1 tbs. cinnamon
1 tbs. unsweetened cocoa

3 tbs. raisins, coarsely chopped
1 cup walnuts, finely chopped

CAKE

3 cups sifted all-purpose flour
1-1/2 tsp. baking powder
1-1/2 tsp. baking soda
1/2 tsp. salt
1 tsp. cinnamon

3/4 cup butter
2 tsp. vanilla extract
1-1/2 cups sugar
3 eggs, unbeaten
2 cups sour cream

58

Mix filling ingredients and set aside. Butter 10-cup bundt pan. To make cake, sift dry ingredients together and set aside. Cream butter. Add vanilla and sugar and beat 1 to 2 minutes. Add eggs one at a time, beating thoroughly after each. Beat at high speed for 1 to 2 minutes until mixture is light and creamy. On lowest speed of mixer alternately add dry ingredients in 3 additions and sour

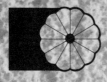

cream in 2 additions. Beat only until smooth after each addition. Spread a thin layer of batter in bottom of pan. Sprinkle with one-third of nut filling. Continue making layers, 4 of batter and 3 of filling. The top layer should be batter. Bake 60 minutes at 375°F. Leave cake in pan only 5 minutes after removing from oven. Invert cake onto plate. Apply glaze on <u>hot</u> cake.

VANILLA GLAZE

2 cups powdered sugar
1 tsp. vanilla extract
3 tbs. milk

Using a rubber spatula, mix sugar with vanilla and 2 tablespoons of milk. Very gradually add more milk until mixture is as thick as heavy cream sauce. Pour glaze on inverted cake. (See Topping Them Off, page 8, for how to keep plate clean.) Let glaze run down sides of cake. Do not attempt to spread it. Sprinkle lightly with cinnamon.

CHERYL'S FAMOUS LEMON CAKE

This is a finely textured cake. Serve with Spiced Iced Coffee, page 61.

3/4 cup butter
1-1/4 cups sugar
8 egg yolks
2-1/2 cups sifted cake flour
3 tsp. baking powder

1/4 tsp. salt
3/4 cup milk
1 tsp. vanilla extract
1 tbs. grated lemon rind
1 tbs. lemon juice

60

Preheat oven to 325°F. Cream butter and sugar until light and fluffy. Beat egg yolks in separate bowl until light-colored. Blend into creamed mixture. Sift cake flour, baking powder and salt together. <u>Resift 3 times.</u> Add sifted ingredients in thirds, alternating with milk. Beat batter thoroughly after each addition. Add vanilla, lemon rind and juice. Beat 2 minutes. Bake in well-greased and floured 10-cup bundt pan for 1 hour or until done. Dust lightly with powdered sugar.

SPICED ICED COFFEE

1 whole cinnamon stick
8 whole cloves
8 cups strong, hot coffee
sugar to taste
cream

Add cinnamon and cloves to hot coffee. Allow to cool, then refrigerate until chilled. Put ice cubes in tall glasses and strain coffee over the ice. Sweeten to taste. Add cream just before serving.

Tube Cakes

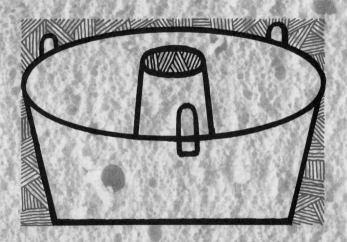

63

GRAND CHAMPION SPONGE CAKE

This tender cake makes an excellent jelly roll base (bake in a 15½ by 10½-inch pan) and substitutes for delicate ladyfingers when cut into thin slices.

1-1/4 cups sifted all-purpose flour
1-1/2 cups sugar
1/2 tsp. baking powder
1/2 tsp. salt

6 eggs, separated
1 tsp. cream of tartar
1/4 cup water
1 tsp. vanilla extract

64

Sift flour, 1 cup sugar, baking powder and salt together. In large bowl, beat egg whites until frothy. Add cream of tartar. Gradually beat in remaining 1/2 cup sugar, a little at a time. Continue beating until whites are glossy and hold stiff peaks. Combine egg yolks, water, vanilla and sifted dry ingredients in a smaller bowl. Beat at medium speed for 4 minutes or until mixture is light and fluffy. Fold yolk mixture gently into egg whites. Turn into an <u>ungreased</u> 10-inch tube pan. Bake at 350°F. 45 minutes or until done. Invert pan to cool. Frost or serve with fruit, ice cream or one of the toppings on page 65.

WHIPPED CREAM TOPPINGS

Instead of frosting, try these refreshingly light toppings on sponge, chiffon, angel food or pound cake slices.

ORANGE WHIP

2 eggs, beaten	1/3 cup orange juice	1 cup heavy cream, whipped
1/2 cup sugar	1 tbs. orange rind	1/2 cup toasted almonds, chopped

Cook eggs, sugar and orange juice over hot water until thick. (It may take as long as 15 minutes). Add rind. Cool. Fold in whipped cream and almonds.

HAWAIIAN FLUFF

3 tbs. powdered sugar	1/4 cup toasted almonds, chopped
1/4 cup crushed pineapple, <u>drained</u>	1 cup heavy cream, whipped

Fold sugar, pineapple and almonds into whipped cream.

ANGEL FOOD CAKE

1-1/4 cups (8 to 10) egg whites
1 cup sifted cake flour
1-1/4 to 1-1/2 cups sugar
1-1/4 tsp. cream of tartar
1/2 tsp. salt
1 tsp. vanilla extract
1/2 to 1 tsp. almond extract

66

Thoroughly wash and dry a 9 or 10-inch tube pan to remove all traces of grease. Preheat oven to 350°F. For best results egg whites should be separated while cold but just before using (no leftovers), and for best volume must be at room temperature (about 70°) when beaten. Sift flour 4 times with 1/2 cup sugar. Beat egg whites until foamy. Add cream of tartar, salt and flavorings. Beat until soft, moist peaks form when beaters are lifted. On high speed beat in remaining sugar, about 2 tablespoons at a time. Continue beating until mixture is firm and holds stiff peaks. Sift about 1/4 cup flour-sugar mixture at a time over the egg whites until all is used. With a rubber scraper fold each addition in

gently until no flour shows, using 8 to 10 complete folding strokes and turning bowl a quarter of a turn after each stroke. Scrape down sides of bowl after last addition and fold 3 or 4 more strokes. Using rubber scraper, carefully push batter into ungreased pan being careful not to stir batter. With a knife or spatula cut carefully through batter, going around the tube 5 or 6 times to break up large air bubbles. Gently level batter and be sure it touches sides of pan and tube. Bake about 1 hour or until top springs back when lightly touched. Deep cracks in top are typical. Remove cake from oven and immediately turn pan upside down. If pan does not have "legs", place tube part over the neck of a funnel or bottle. Let cake hang until completely cooled.

HEAVENLY ICE CREAM LAYER CAKE

A dessert that is ready and waiting for the meal's finish.

1 Grand Champion Sponge Cake, page 64, or Angel Food, page 66, or
Buttermilk Pound Cake, page 71
1 qt. (use 1 or 2 flavors) Ice cream, softened
1 cup heavy cream
1 tbs. sugar
1 tsp. vanilla extract
1 bag (4 ozs.) shredded coconut

Cut tube cake horizontally into 3 layers. Spread softened ice cream between layers. Place cake in freezer to harden. Whip cream. Add sugar and vanilla. Frost top and sides of cake. Cover with coconut and return to freezer until whipped cream is hard. Serve without thawing. Slicing will be easier if knife is dipped in hot water for each cut. Makes 16 to 20 servings.

ANGEL ALEXANDER

This simple angel food cake is enhanced by creme de cacao.

1 baked angel food cake still in pan
3 tbs. light cream
3/4 cup dark creme de cacao
1 cup heavy cream, whipped
2 tbs. powdered sugar
shaved semisweet or milk chocolate

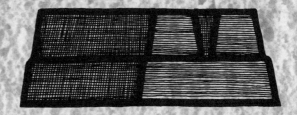

69

Early in the day bake an angel food cake from scratch or from a mix. About 4 hours before serving, with a thin skewer (the kind you use for kebabs) make many holes of varying depths in cake. Combine cream and creme de cacao. Pour half of mixture into holes. Let cake set in pan for 2 hours. Invert cake onto serving plate. Make more holes in top and pour in remaining creme de cacao mixture. Whip cream and sugar until stiff. Frost cake with whipped cream and garnish with shaved chocolate. Chill at least 1 hour before serving.

BUTTERSCOTCH CHIFFON CAKE

2-1/4 cups sifted cake flour
3 tsp. baking powder
1 tsp. salt
2 cups firmly-packed brown sugar
1/2 cup cooking oil

5 egg yolks, unbeaten
3/4 cup cold water
2 tsp. vanilla
1 cup egg whites (7 or 8)
1/2 cup cream of tartar

70   Preheat oven to 325°F. Sift flour, baking powder and salt together into large bowl. Stir in brown sugar until blended. Make a well in center of dry ingredients and add in order, the oil, egg yolks, water and vanilla. Beat with wooden spoon until smooth. In large bowl beat egg whites and cream of tartar until stiff peaks form. Pour egg yolk mixture gradually over egg whites gently folding in with rubber scraper just until blended. Pour batter into <u>ungreased</u> 10-inch tube pan. Bake at 325°F. 55 minutes, then increase temperature to 350°F. and bake 10 to 15 minutes longer, or until top of cake springs back when lightly touched. Remove from oven and immediately turn cake upside down. Let cake hang until completely cooled. Frost with Penuche Frosting, page 41.

BUTTERMILK POUND CAKE

1/2 cup butter	1 cup buttermilk
2-1/2 cups sugar	2 tsps. vanilla extract
4 eggs	1 tsp. almond extract
3 cups sifted flour	grated peel of 1 large orange
1/4 tsp. baking soda	grated peel of 1 small lemon

Cream butter. Gradually add sugar, beating until mixture is light and fluffy. Add eggs one at a time. Beat well after each addition. Combine buttermilk, vanilla, almond and peel. Sift flour with soda. Beat into creamed mixture alternately with buttermilk mixture, beginning and ending with dry ingredients. Place batter in greased and floured 10-inch tube pan or 2 4 by 8-inch loaf pans. Bake at 350°F. for 1 hour or until done. Cool 5 minutes in pan. Turn out on rack to continue cooling.

PUMPKIN CAKE

In summer we'd sip Cafe Orange with slightly warm cake.

3 cups sifted flour
2 cups sugar
1 tsp. salt
1 tsp. cinnamon
2 tsp. baking powder
2 tsp. baking soda
1 cup Wesson oil
4 eggs, unbeaten
2 cups canned pumpkin or fresh pumpkin, cooked and mashed
1 cup chopped nuts
3/4 cup chocolate chips (optional)

Sift dry ingredients together. Add remaining ingredients in order. Mix well. Bake in greased 10-inch tube pan at 375°F. for 1 hour. Serve plain or with whipped cream.

# CAFE ORANGE

crushed or chopped ice
cold extra-strong coffee
2 tbs. sugar
1/4 cup Cointreau or Grand Marnier
1/4 tsp. grated orange rind
1 cup milk

73

Put ice in cup to half-cup level. Fill to top with coffee. Combine with remaining ingredients in blender container and blend at high speed until foamy. Serve in tall glasses, garnished with orange slice. Makes 2 servings.

PINEAPPLE FLUFF CAKE

A super-light cake that invites different frostings.

6 eggs, separated
1/4 tsp. salt
1-1/2 cups sugar
1 tbs. lemon juice
1/2 cup unsweetened pineapple juice
1-1/2 cups sifted cake flour
1 tsp. baking powder

74

Beat egg whites with salt until soft peaks form. Gradually beat in 3/4 cup sugar. Beat egg yolks and remaining 3/4 cup sugar until thick. Add lemon and pineapple juice. Beat until sugar is dissolved. Add flour which has been sifted with baking powder. Fold in egg whites. Bake at 325°F. one hour or until done. Invert to cool. Frost with Cream Cheese Frosting, page 21, or the topping of your choice.

PECAN TORTE

5 eggs, separated
1 cup sugar
1/2 cup sifted flour
1 tbs. instant coffee powder
1/2 cup pecans, finely ground
1 pt. heavy cream
4 tbs. powdered sugar
1 tbs. sherry, optional

Beat egg whites until fluffy peaks form. Gradually add sugar, beating after each addition. Beat egg yolks until lemon-colored and thick. Gently fold the <u>yolks into the whites.</u> Mix flour, coffee and nuts together. Carefully fold into egg mixture until no dark streams remain. Spoon batter into greased and floured 10-inch tube pan. Bake at 325°F. 55 to 60 minutes. Let cool and remove from pan. Cut into 3 or 4 layers. Fill and frost with slightly sweetened whipped cream or a favorite light-textured frosting. Chill. Makes 10 to 12 servings.

Springform Cakes

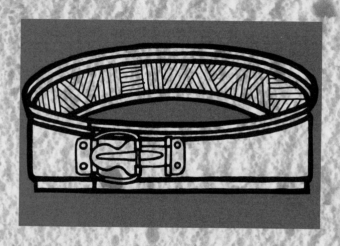

THE PEDESTAL CAKE

This shallow cake sits high and proud on an antique glass pedestal.

fine dry bread crumbs
6 ozs. semisweet chocolate, coarsely broken
3/4 cup butter
2/3 cup sugar
6 eggs, separated
1-1/4 cups finely ground blanched, unsalted almonds
1/8 tsp. salt
Pedestal Cake Icing, page 80

Place oven rack in lower third of the oven. Butter an 8-inch springform pan and line the bottom with buttered waxed paper. Dust with fine, dry bread crumbs. Set aside. Melt chocolate in a bowl over hot water. Do not stir. Cream butter in small mixer bowl. Add sugar and beat at moderate speed 2 to 3 minutes. Add yolks one at a time, beating until each is thoroughly blended. Beat in chocolate. On lowest mixer speed gradually beat in almonds. Transfer to a

large bowl. Beat egg whites with salt until stiff, but not dry. Stir a large spoonful of whites into chocolate mixture. In three additions, fold in the remaining whites. Fold gently until there is no trace of whites. Turn mixture into crumb-lined pan. Bake 20 minutes at 375°F. Reduce temperature to 350°F. and bake an additional 50 minutes. Do not overbake. Cake will remain soft and moist in the center. Wet and slightly wring out a folded towel and place it on a smooth surface. Remove springform pan from oven and place it directly on towel. Let stand 20 minutes. Remove sides of springform. Place a rack over the cake and carefully invert cake and rack. Remove bottom of springform and paper lining. Cover with second rack and invert again to cool right side up. The cake will be about 1-3/4 inches high. When cool, transfer to serving plate, bottom up. Frost with Pedestal Cake Icing.

PEDESTAL CAKE ICING

1/2 cup heavy cream
2 tsp. instant coffee powder
8 ozs. semisweet chocolate, coarsely broken

Scald cream in saucepan over moderate heat until it begins to form small bubbles around the edges. Over heat, add instant coffee and stir briskly with whisk until dissolved. Add chocolate. After 1 minute remove from heat and stir until mixture is smooth. Set saucepan in cold water to stop the cooking. Let mixture stand at room temperature for 15 minutes or more, stirring occasionally until it reaches room temperature. Stir (<u>do not beat</u>) mixture and pour over top of cake. Use a spatula to smooth the top, letting icing run down the sides. (See Topping Them Off, page 8, for advice about keeping the serving plate clean). Cake serves 12 to 16, depending on the number of chocolate lovers.

LEMONY APPLE CAKE

Bake this cake several days before serving to allow the lemon flavor to develop.

1/2 cup soft butter	1 cup sifted flour
1/3 cup sugar	grated rind of 2 lemons
2 eggs, unbeaten	5 apples, peeled
1/3 cup lemon juice	3 tbs. melted butter
1/8 tsp. salt	5 tbs. sugar

Cream butter and sugar. Add eggs one at a time, beating thoroughly after each addition. Add 1 tablespoon lemon juice and salt. Gradually add flour, beating until mixture is smooth. Fold in 1 tablespoon lemon rind. Spread batter in buttered springform pan. Cut apples into 1/8-inch slices. Toss with remaining lemon juice and arrange evenly over batter. Mix melted butter and remaining lemon rind. Spoon over apples and sprinkle with sugar. Bake at 350°F. for 1 hour or until apples are golden brown. Cool in pan on rack.

SWEDISH ALMOND COFFEE ROUND

At home, we'd always "cook coffee" to go with this nutty marzipan cake. The Boiled Egg Coffee recipe is on page 84. It's delicious...try it!

SPECIAL PASTRY

5 tbs. sugar
1-1/2 cups <u>unsifted</u> all-purpose flour
1/2 cup butter, cut in small pieces
1 egg yolk

Stir sugar and flour together. Cut butter pieces into flour mixture, then rub with fingers until evenly blended. Stir in egg yolk with fork. Compress mixture with hands to form a smooth ball. Cover and chill if made ahead, but use at room temperature. Press dough up about 1 inch on sides of 8-inch springform pan and pat firmly on bottom. Filling goes into <u>unbaked</u> shell.

MARZIPAN FILLING

3/4 cup (8 oz. pkg.) almond paste
2 tbs. sugar
2 tbs. all-purpose flour
2 eggs, unbeaten
1 egg white, unbeaten
1/4 tsp. almond extract
2 tbs. milk
1 cup <u>unsifted</u> powdered sugar

Break almond paste into small pieces and blend smoothly with sugar and flour. Add whole eggs and blend. Add egg white. Blend well. Stir in almond extract. Pour into pastry lined pan. Bake at 325°F. for 1 hour and 10 minutes or until top is golden brown. Let cool 5 minutes. Glaze with mixture of milk and powdered sugar. When cool, remove pan rim. Cut in 8 to 10 wedges.

BOILED EGG COFFEE

Albumen from the egg white and calcium from the shell cooked in the coffee produces a clear, but strong brew. It will reheat without becoming stronger or bitter. Economical, too, as you use slightly less coffee than with standard coffee makers.

6 cups	12 cups	18 cups
1/3 of egg mixture	2/3 of egg mixture	all of egg mixture
6 cups boiling water	12 cups boiling water	18 cups boiling water
1/2 cup coffee	1 cup coffee	1-1/2 cups coffee
1 tbs. cold water	1 tbs. cold water	3 tbs. cold water
dash salt	dash salt	dash salt
1/4 cup cold water	1/4 cup cold water	1/2 cup cold water

Break 1 egg into a small bowl. Beat well with fork. Add broken and crushed shell. Measure out amount needed. Cover and refrigerate any remaining mixture for later use. Boil water in coffee pot. Place coffee in small bowl. Add cold

water, salt and desired amount of egg mixture, including some shell. Stir until thoroughly mixed. Add mixture to boiling water, stirring gently. Bring to a boil. Watch carefully to avoid foaming or boiling over. Lower heat and cook 2 to 3 minutes, stirring occasionally. Add cold water. Turn off heat. Let coffee settle for about 5 to 10 minutes. Pour through tea strainer directly into cups or into a serving pot.

85

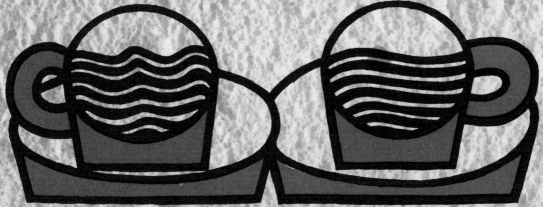

FINNIE'S SECRET CAKE

Soda crackers are the baffling ingredient in this elegant dessert.

22 square (7/8 cup crushed) saltines
4 eggs, separated
3/4 cup sugar
1 cup chopped walnuts
1 tsp. vanilla extract
1/4 tsp. cream of tartar
1/2 cup raspberry jam
6 macaroon cookies
1/4 cup gin, Kirsch or other liquor
1/2 cup heavy cream, whipped

86

Finely crush, but do not pulverize crackers. Beat yolks and sugar together. Blend in nuts and vanilla. Add cracker crumbs. Beat egg whites with cream of tartar until stiff, but not dry. Fold into cracker mixture. Pour batter into greased springform pan. Bake at 350°F. 20 to 30 minutes. When cool, spread raspberry

jam over top. Dip macaroons in liquor (or water), shake briefly, and place in circle on top of cake. Place one macaroon in the center. Spread barely sweetened (or unsweetened) whipped cream over top of cake. Chill. Makes 12 to 14 servings.

LIZ'S CHEESE CAKE

1/4 lb. (9 double) graham crackers
2 tbs. sugar
1-1/2 tsp. cinnamon
6 tbs. melted butter
3 pkgs. (8 oz. ea.) cream cheese
1 cup sugar

3 eggs
1/2 tsp. vanilla
1 pt. sour cream
3 tbs. sugar
1/2 tsp. vanilla extract

88

Roll graham crackers into fine crumbs. Mix crumbs, 2 tablespoons sugar, cinnamon and melted butter together. Press onto bottom of a 10-inch springform pan. Set aside. Beat cheese until creamy. Add sugar gradually and beat well. Add eggs one at a time, beating after each addition. Add vanilla. Pour on top of unbaked crust. Bake at 375°F. 20 to 25 minutes or until brown around the edges. Remove cheesecake from oven and increase temperature to 500°F. Whip sour cream, 3 tablespoons sugar, and vanilla together lightly. Pour over baked cheesecake. Put back into oven for 5 minutes. Cool at room temperature. Cut in small pieces. Makes 16 to 20 servings.

Index

books designed with giving in mind

Pies & Cakes
Yogurt
The Ground Beef Cookbook
Cocktails & Hors d'Oeuvres
Salads & Casseroles
Kid's Party Book
Pressure Cooking
Food Processor Cookbook
Peanuts & Popcorn
Kid's Pets Book
Make It Ahead
    French Cooking
Soups & Stews
Crepes & Omelets

Microwave Cooking
Vegetable Cookbook
Kid's Arts and Crafts
Bread Baking
The Crockery Pot Cookbook
Kid's Garden Book
Classic Greek Cooking
Low Carbohydrate Cookbook
Kid's Cookbook
Italian
Cheese Guide & Cookbook
Miller's German
Quiche & Souffle
To My Daughter, With Love

Natural Foods
Chinese Vegetarian
The Jewish Cookbook
Working Couples
Mexican
Sunday Breakfast
Fisherman's Wharf Cookbook
Charcoal Cookbook
Ice Cream Cookbook
Blender Cookbook
The Wok, a Chinese Cookbook
Japanese Country
Fondue Cookbook

from nitty gritty productions

TO MY MOM
who taught me two important things about cooking: use only the best ingredients, "You're putting it into yourself," she'd say; and take plenty of time. "If the phone rings, don't answer. If the doorbell chimes, call that they should come in and sit a spell."
AND TO HERTHA, ROGER AND PAUL.

Pies

by
Arlene Mueller

Happy baking!
Arlene Mueller

Illustrated by Mike Nelson

ISBN 0-911954-48-1
Library of Congress Catalog Card Number: 78-52771

Table of Contents

A Pie for Every Season

Sundays were pie days at our house. Early in the morning we'd hear the rhythmic thump of the rolling pin, and soon baked pies were cooling on the wooden cupboard - in summertime before the open window with a slight breeze billowing the curtains; in wintertime in front of a frosted window with snow flurries blowing outside. Different kinds of pies helped us observe the constant cycle of changing seasons in our midwestern life.

In the fall we had apple pies with cheese or brandied raisins or hot lemon sauce. The Halloween jack-o-lantern kept its shell, but gave us its meat for several spicy pies.

Christmas pies were usually sour cream raisin, pecan or the traditional mincemeat, which was made in the crock with real meat and plenty of brandy.

Easter meant an extra-high lemon meringue pie. Its golden yellow filling blended with the blooming daffodils. Strawberry-rhubarb pies came with the spring, as soon as the rhubarb sprouted its tender pink stalks. Who saw to it that the strawberries would appear at the same time?

Early summer meant peach pies and cobblers. Little blueberries picked in

the north woods were baked in flaky crusts and needed no topping. On summer evenings while crickets chirped contentedly in the garden we sipped ice tea, slightly minted, and ate pie made of ice cream crusts and berries.

Each season held its own special treat.

The Right Equipment

Certain pieces of equipment are essential for successful, frustration-free pie baking, while others are useful but not absolutely necessary.

Standard measuring cups and spoons are a must for perfect results and so is a large flat area where you have plenty of room for rolling out the crust. If you don't already have a pastry cloth and stockinet for the rolling pin, invest in a set soon. They make rolling much easier by preventing crust (or cookie dough) from sticking without the addition of too much extra flour. Work a little flour into the pastry cloth before each use. Shake the cloth and stockinet well after using and store them in a plastic zip-loc bag with the floured side folded in. Wash occasionally in hot soapy water, rinse well and hang to dry.

When choosing a rolling pin, carefully select one that is the right weight and length for you. They come in metal, glass, plastic and wood, and those with ball bearing handles are easier to use.

The most popular size pie plate is 9 inches. They also come in 8 and 10 inch sizes, but are not as readily available. I prefer glass, although dull, anodized aluminum or other darkened metals work well since they absorb heat and produce well-browned bottom crusts. Never use throw-away, shiny aluminum

pans as they reflect heat and result in soggy bottom crusts. Deep-dish pies and cobblers can be baked in almost any casserole-type dish and do not require a rim for an edging.

A <u>pastry blender</u> cuts fat into flour quickly and evenly, but <u>two knives</u> work fine (see page 12) if a pastry blender is not available. And always place a pie or pie shell on a cooling rack as soon as they are taken from the oven to prevent the crust from becoming soggy as it cools.

An <u>extra set of beaters</u> used only for egg whites is great to have when making meringues and chiffon pies (angel food cakes, too). Total absence of oil is necessary when beating egg whites. If you aren't lucky enough to have extra beaters, thoroughly wash the ones you have in hot soapy water and rinse with boiling water before using and you'll never have any trouble.

Although not essential there are a few "gadgets" which I enjoy using, mainly for decorative purposes. A <u>pastry wheel</u> quickly makes an attractive finish on the outer edge of a pie as well as decorative strips for lattice tops, and a <u>sealer-cutter</u> produces an attractive, firmly-sealed edge.

I have two glass, <u>barbecue-size salt and pepper shakers</u> with wide mouths

which I find extremely handy. One is for the ice water or milk used in making the pie crust. Sprinkling distributes the liquid more evenly than pouring. For faster measuring, carefully mark off the tablespoons on the outside on the shaker, using paint or nail polish. I keep cinnamon-sugar in the other shaker for sprinkling on pie tops, cookies, etc.

   Always have <u>plastic wrap</u> and <u>waxed paper</u> handy and if you have a <u>pastry brush</u>, I guarantee you'll use it many times.

5

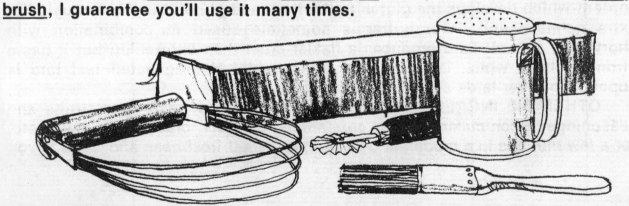

The Right Ingredients

FLOUR - All purpose flour is best to use in making pie crust. Cake flour is too fine and whole wheat flour does not give the same flaky results.

FAT - The most commonly used fat for making pie crust is hydrogenated vegetable shortening (Crisco, Spry, Snowdrift, etc.) because it has a bland flavor and an ideal consistency for blending with the flour. It yields a more tender product than butter or margarine because they have a higher moisture content which develops the gluten in the flour and gluten toughens crust. For extra richness and flavor butter is sometimes used in combination with shortening or lard. Lard produces a flakier crust than shortening but it has a stronger flavor which is sometimes undesirable. Hydrogenated leaf lard is superior to other lards and is recommended.

OTHER PIE INGREDIENTS - Use whole milk and fresh eggs, fruits and seasonings. When making variety crusts toast the nuts, crackers, cookies, etc. for a few minutes in a moderate oven to give added freshness and extra flavor.

Understanding Pie Crust

The ingredients used in making pie crust - fat, flour, liquid and salt - couldn't be simpler, but what the crust will look and taste like depends on how these basics go together. And that depends entirely on the baker.

Rather than describe the process scientifically, I'd like you to "see" what happens . . .

Picture a mound of soft flour. Add cold fat to it and quickly slash through the flour with two knives, or a pastry blender, until the little balls of flour-covered fat appear. Gradually add cold liquid and toss until the dough is moist enough to stick together without crumbling. Shape the dough into a patty and chill if possible. Roll it thin, place it in a pie plate and pop it into a very hot oven.

Whooooooooooosh - now the magic happens. The still-chilled little fat balls burst out in all directions, making a flaky crust with lots of air spaces.

This will happen if you treat your dough right - keep it cold, handle it gently and work quickly.

COLDNESS

It's important to keep everything chilled throughout the preparation of pie crust. For flaky crust you must prevent the fat from warming up and melting into the flour. I keep my shortening (Crisco) in the refrigerator, and before starting to make crust I chill the mixing bowl, knives or pastry blender, and even the rolling pin, for a short time.

If I'm using water, I place it in the freezer for a few minutes, or add an ice cube. When using milk, I don't pour it until I'm just ready to use it, and I sometimes even add an ice cube to chill it slightly more.

If you must answer the phone or pause even for a few minutes during your crust preparation, quickly return everything to the refrigerator. And, whenever possible, chill the dough for a few minutes between mixing and rolling.

After you have rolled the bottom crust and fitted it into the pie plate, place it in the refrigerator until you have rolled out the top crust and prepared the filling. If time allows, chill the <u>unfilled</u> shell for at least an hour before baking. Chilling overnight is even better when possible. <u>Never chill a pie after it is filled.</u>

Remember, once a pie is filled it's right quick into the oven or the bottom crust will become soggy.

GENTLENESS

Gentle treatment in both mixing stages is important when making pie crust. In the first stage, when combining the flour and fat, use cutting motions, never stir or mash. Remember, you want to avoid fully combining these ingredients. They should be in particles about the size of peas.

In the second stage of mixing, lightly toss the flour-fat mixture as you add the liquid. It is essential to incorporate air as it inhibits the development of gluten (which toughens crust) and makes light, tender pastry.

Roll the dough out with firm but gentle strokes. Carefully ease the crust into the pie plate and form the edging with a light touch. Gentle treatment allows the fat particles every chance to burst out when placed in a hot oven.

QUICKNESS

The reason for working quickly is to maintain the chill of the fat. If you want a light, flaky pie crust you must do everything possible to avoid having the fat soften or melt into the flour.

Making Pie Crust

MOM'S FLAKY CRUST - A step-by-step demonstration

This is my favorite recipe and the one I use most often.

<u>9 inch, 2-crust</u>
2 cups sifted all-purpose flour
2/3 cup Crisco shortening
1/2 tsp. salt
4 to 7 tbs. cold milk

<u>9 inch, 1-crust</u>
1 cup sifted all-purpose flour
1/3 cup Crisco shortening
1/4 tsp. salt
3 to 5 tbs. cold milk

MIXING

Measure ingredients, and assemble utensils - mixing bowl, 2 table knives or a pastry blender, a lightly floured pastry cloth, stockinet, a rolling pin and a pastry brush. Chill all ingredients, the mixing bowl and knives for several minutes before starting.

Sift flour and salt together into chilled bowl. Add half of cold shortening and cut quickly with knives moving in parallel motions until shortening and flour form into small balls. Add remaining shortening and cut in until particles are the size of small peas.

Sprinkle 1/2 of the liquid over flour mixture. Lightly toss with a fork. Add 1/4 more liquid and repeat procedure. Gently squeeze a fistful of dough. If it sticks together, but does not crumble, and is smooth and pliable, it is ready for rolling. If it doesn't stick together, add liquid, a few drops at a time until it does. You may not always need all of the liquid called for, since flour absorbs liquid in varying amounts. Stop adding liquid immediately if dough approaches stickiness.

Note - If dough is "sticky" and clings to your fingers, gradually sift several tablespoons of flour onto the dough and press gently until it loses stickiness.

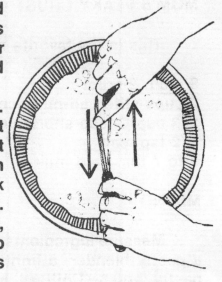

12

Avoid this step if possible, as any additional handling will produce a crust which is less than best.

If you are making a double-crust pie, shape dough into 2 flat patties about 1/4 to 1/2 inch thick and 5 to 6 inches in diameter. Shape single-crust dough into one patty. Chill at least 10 minutes if time allows (longer is better). Otherwise, skip the chilling and roll out immediately.

ROLLING

If the dough has been chilling for considerable time, remove it from the refrigerator several minutes before rolling to allow it to soften, otherwise it may require excess handling.

Lay patty on floured pastry cloth. Be sure there are no cracks on the outer edges of the patty and that it is no more than 1/2 inch thick. If needed, flatten gently with fingers.

Take a firm grip on both ends of rolling pin and come down on the middle of patty. Roll from center <u>away from you</u> coming up with a sweep at the edge of

dough. (Don't worry, you'll soon develop a real flourish!) Moving pastry cloth in a clockwise direction, continue rolling, always away from you. <u>Never</u> pull the pin toward you or roll across the entire surface, as this stretches the dough. (The more the dough is stretched the more it will shrink during baking.)

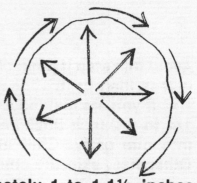

14   Roll as directed until you have a circle approximately 1 to 1-1½ inches larger than the pie plate. If the dough breaks, squeeze the tear together gently

with fingertips moistened with cold milk or water. If a large crack occurs, take a "patch" from the outer edge of dough that exceeds the circle size. Lay it lightly over the hole or crack and carefully roll over it with freshly floured pin.

If it appears that the dough will stick to the cloth when being lifted into the plate, carefully loosen the edges with a spatula or knife.

LIFTING DOUGH INTO PIE PLATE

There are different ways you can successfully lift the dough into a pie plate:

Place the rolling pin at the edge of dough nearest to you. Gently wrap the dough around the pin and roll it away from you until the entire crust is on the pin. Place pie plate where the dough was and roll pin backwards, unrolling the crust into the plate. A long rolling pin is necessary for this method, or you'll have difficulty keeping the edges from crumbling off.

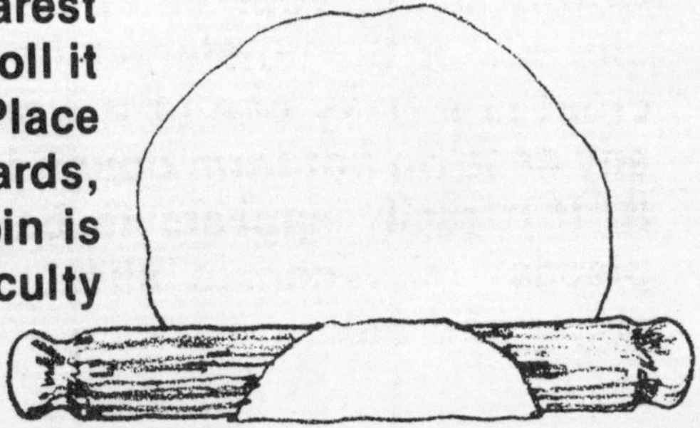

Using the pastry cloth, lift the pastry-half nearest to you and flip it carefully onto the other half. Carefully lift and lay folded edge in the center of pie plate. Flip outer half back toward you.

Fold circle of dough gently into quarters and transfer to pie plate, placing point in center. Gently unfold.

16

If crust tears as you are lifting it into the plate, don't panic. Most likely the tears will be small ones. Gently begin your patch-up work by pressing cracks closed with moistened fingertips. (Remember your crust is a flaky one or it wouldn't be falling apart.) In any case do not form dough into patty again and re-roll it. If it really appears to be beyond repair, place the pieces on a cookie sheet, sprinkle with cinnamon-sugar and bake.

Once you have the dough in the pie plate, without stretching, ease from center of pan out to rim. Use fingers to fit the dough onto sides of plate. Then lift plate up a little and drop gently onto the flat surface. This will settle the crust evenly into pie plate with a minimum of stretching. Using scissors or a knife, trim dough evenly around rim leaving a 1-inch overhang.

EDGING

When making a single crust pie or baked pie shell, it is at this point, after the crust is in the plate, that you will decide about the type of edging to make. If the dough has a tendency to crumble you can guess that it won't cooperate for any fancy finish, so a simple one such as pressing with a fork, is a good choice. If the dough is soft and pliable, do something decorative. Fold overhang under and finish as desired.

BAKING A ONE-CRUST PIE

After the crust is in the pie plate, but before it is chilled, prick the bottom and sides of the shell several times with a fork, paying particular attention to the indentation where sides and bottom of the plate meet. Pricking allows steam to escape and helps prevent bubbles from forming and lessens shrinking. Chill at least 10 minutes, or longer if posssible. If desired, you can also use pie weights (small metal balls) or dry beans or rice in the bottom of the shell to help reduce shrinking. (The beans and rice can be used over and over for years.) Just before baking, butter a piece of lightweigh aluminum foil the approximate size of the

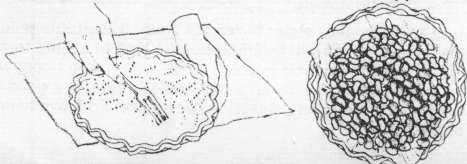

shell. Place it buttered side down in chilled pastry shell. Fill with weights. Bake in preheated, 450° F. oven 7 to 8 minutes, until partially set but still soft. Remove foil and weights and prick dough again with fork. Bake a few minutes longer until shell is lightly browned and crisp. Watch carefully.

BAKING A TWO-CRUST PIE

Do not prick the bottom of a double-crust pie. Instead, using a pastry brush, paint the bottom of the shell with slightly beaten egg white to help prevent a soggy crust. Place in refrigerator while you roll out the top crust.

The top crust is rolled the same as the bottom one, except it should be about an inch smaller. Make 6 to 8, 2-inch slashes or cut decorative vents in top. Chill while you prepare filling.

Fill shell and trim away most of overhang leaving dough about 1/4-inch wider than rim. Moisten rim of bottom crust. Quickly center top crust over filling. Press edges firmly to seal. Tuck edges of top crust under bottom crust edges. Flute as desired.

If recipe calls for it, sprinkle the top of the pie with sugar or brush with cold milk to create a golden tone (or "bloom" as the old-timers call it) as it bakes. Do not brush edges as they will brown nicely without help.

Place pie in preheated oven on the middle rack. Check occasionally to be sure crust is not overbrowning. Rotate the pie if browning is uneven. If edges of pie become too brown, place a narrow strip of foil over edges. Bake each pie according to directions in the recipe you are following.

ELECTRIC MIXER CRUST

Making pie crust with an electric mixer is fast and easy. The fat and flour are blended so quickly there's no time for the fat to become warm and melt into the flour. No special recipe is needed, just use your favorite one calling for solid shortening or butter or a combination of the two.

Cut chilled, firm shortening into small pieces. If it begins to soften in the process, return the pieces to refrigerator or freezer until firm again. Place flour and salt in mixer bowl. Add pieces of cold shortening. With mixer on medium speed, mix fat and flour until particles are the size of small peas. Be careful not to overmix and soften shortening. Mixture should be light and dry. Turn mixer off. Add most of the liquid, holding back a tablespoon or two. Turn mixer on for a few seconds until dough gathers in blades of beater. Add more liquid by drops to the unblended bits. Scrape dough out of mixing bowl onto a flat working surface. Gather dough into a ball. Divide and flatten into patties and smooth edges so there are no cracks. Wrap in plastic and chill until ready to roll.

FOOD PROCESSOR CRUST

For easiest mixing, use a recipe calling for no more than 2 cups of flour. With steel or plastic blade in place, add flour, salt and fat, which has been cut into small pieces, to processor bowl. Process using "on-off" turns until particles are in small (about 1/4 inch) pieces. With processor running, add liquid through feed tube. Stop adding liquid when dough becomes lumpy. (You will probably have a little liquid left.) Let processor run a few seconds longer until dough gathers into a ball, then stop immediately. Remove dough and shape into two flattened rounds, using a little extra flour if necessary. Wrap in plastic and chill until ready to roll.

23

NEVER-FAIL CRUST

Never chill this pastry before rolling.

9 inch, 2-crust	9 inch, 1 crust
2 cups sifted all-purpose flour	1 cup sifted all-purpose flour
1 tsp. salt	1/2 tsp. salt
1/2 cup Wesson oil, or corn oil	1/4 cup Wesson oil, or corn oil
1/4 cup cold milk	2 tbs. cold milk

24

Gently stir ingredients together. Form into one or two balls depending on which recipe you made. Do not chill. Flatten each ball and shape into a circle. Place between two pieces of waxed paper. Roll out to desired size. Peel off top piece of paper. Place pie plate, upside down, on pastry. Holding pastry and plate together, turn plate right side up. Gently peel off remaining waxed paper. Carefully fit into pan without stretching. Finish edges as desired. Chill until needed. If making a two-crust pie, roll second ball. Leave crust flat and between pieces of waxed paper. Chill while preparing filling. For more detailed information see Making Pie Crust, page 11.

LEMON-EGG CRUST

A firm pastry that works well for fancy edgings and tops. If you are using only one crust, wrap the other one well and refrigerate or freeze.

9 inch, 2-crust
2 cups sifted all-purpose flour
1 tsp. salt
2/3 cup Crisco
1 egg, slightly beaten
2 tbs. cold water
2 tsp. lemon juice

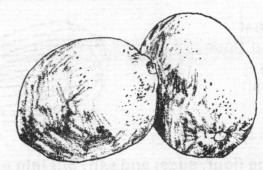

Sift flour and salt into mixing bowl. Cut in shortening until particles are the size of small peas. Combine egg, water and lemon juice. Sprinkle over dry ingredients, tossing with fork until mixture is moist enough to hold together. If more water is needed, add it a few drops at a time. Form into two flat patties about 1/2 inch thick. Refrigerate at least 10 minutes (longer, if possible) before rolling. For more detailed information see Making Pie Crust, page 11.

SHORT-CUT PASTRY

This crust by-passes the rolling pin. It tastes especially good with fruit fillings.

9 inch, 2-crust
2 cups sifted flour
2 tsp. sugar
1-1/4 tsp. salt
2/3 cup oil
3 tbs. milk

Combine flour, sugar and salt. Sift into a 9-inch pie plate. Whip oil and milk together with a whisk. Pour over flour mixture. Stir with a fork until all flour is moistened. Save out about one third of dough for top of pie. Press remaining dough evenly in plate, covering bottom and sides. Add fruit filling. Crumble remaining dough over filling to make top crust. Bake as the pie filling requires.

GRAHAM CRACKER CRUST # 1

9 inch, 1-crust
7/8 cup (1 cup less 2 tbs.) sifted all-purpose flour
3/4 tsp. salt
1/3 cup Crisco shortening
2 tbs. water
1/3 cup finely-rolled graham cracker crumbs

Sift flour and salt together twice. Cut in shortening. Gradually add water. Toss and stir until mixture is smooth. Gather into ball and refrigerate overnight. Next day, sprinkle graham cracker crumbs on an unfloured pastry board. Flatten dough and roll to 1/8-inch thickness. The cracker crumbs should be only on the bottom side of the dough. Arrange crust, crumb side down, in pie plate. If crust is to be filled before it is baked, wait an hour before filling and baking. Bake as pie filling requires. If baking crust without filling, bake at 425° F. 20 minutes. Allow baked shell to set an hour before filling.

GRAHAM CRACKER CRUST # 2

<u>9 inch</u>, <u>1-crust</u>
1-1/3 cups graham cracker crumbs (16 to 18 2-1/2 in. crackers)
1 tbs. flour
1/4 cup sugar
1/3 cup soft butter
1/4 tsp. nutmeg
28 1/8 tsp. salt

Combine cracker crumbs, flour, sugar, butter, and nutmeg. Blend until crumbly. Save out 1/3 cup crumbs to use on top of pie if desired. Press remaining crumbs evenly on bottom and sides of pie plate, making sure the thickness is not excessive in the crease. Bake at 375°F, 8 minutes, or until lightly browned. Cool before filling.

MERINGUE PIE SHELL

So pretty for special occasions and easy to make if you know the "tricks" to being successful with meringue shells. Choose a cool, dry day void of humidity and have egg whites at room temperature. Wash and rinse beaters and bowl in hot water. Even a speck of oil can ruin a meringue. And most importantly, the sugar must be completely dissolved. Test a little of the meringue between your fingers ... if grainy, beat until it is smooth. The total beating time will take several minutes on high speed.

3 egg whites
1/4 tsp. cream of tartar
1/8 tsp. salt
3/4 cup sugar

Combine egg whites (room temperature), cream of tartar and salt. Beat until frothy. Gradually add sugar and beat until stiff peaks form. Continue beating on high speed until sugar is dissolved. Test between fingers until no longer grainy. Spread over bottom and sides of a well-greased pie plate. Build sides high. Bake

at 275° F. 1 hour, or until light brown and crisp to the touch. Turn oven off and open door. Leave until cool. Don't be upset if the shell cracks and falls - that's quite normal.

Note - For individual shells or special shapes, spread heavy brown paper on a baking sheet. Draw outline of desired size and shape. Spoon meringue mixture inside of outline. Shape with back of spoon. Build up sides and leave depression in middle for filling. Bake as directed. Remove from paper when cool.

ICE CREAM PIE SHELL

1 pt. slightly-softened ice cream

Cut ice cream in slices about 1/2-inch thick. Cover bottom of pie plate with as many slices as necessary. Next lay slices around plate to form sides. Fill in holes as needed. Smooth whole shell with back of spoon. Place in freezer until firm. Fill with fresh fruit and top with a sauce or whipped cream. . .or both!

TART SHELLS

Lemon-Egg Crust, page 25, works well for tart shells because it is firm and molds easily. Some tart shells are baked filled; some are filled after they are baked. Watch closely during baking as they bake quickly and can easily overbrown. Always cool baked shells before filling. Tart fillings can be made from most pie recipes, except for custard fillings which are best left as full-size pies.

PETAL SHELLS - Use 3-inch muffin tins, or custard cups turned upside down. Roll dough into a 14 by 10-inch rectangle, 1/8 inch thick. Cut 6, 4-1/2 inch squares. Prick with fork. Drape pastry squares over custard cups and make pleats with extra crust between each 2 points to make pastry fit cup tightly, or fit pastry squares into muffin cups letting corners stand up in a petal effect. Bake 12 to 15 minutes at 450° F.

CUP SHELLS - Roll out dough to 1/8 inch thickness. Cut into 4-1/2 inch circles for custard cups or 1 inch larger than whatever dish you are using. Drape pastry circles over cups, pleating dough to fit tightly. Prick with fork. Place cups, crust-side up on cookie sheet. Bake 8 to 10 minutes at 475° F.

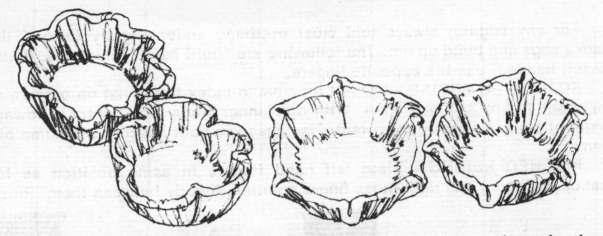

ALUMINUM FOIL SHELLS - Cut 6, 6-inch circles of heavy duty aluminum foil. Prepare Lemon-Egg Crust, page 25, for a 2-crust pie. Divide dough into 6 pieces. Shape into balls, flatten and roll each into a 6-inch circle, 1/8 inch thick. Lay crust circles on top of foil circles. Shape foil and crust together into tart shells by turning up a 1-inch (or more) rim and finish edges. My two favorite edgings are scalloped and pinched. (See Decorative Edgings, page 34.)

DECORATIVE EDGINGS

For any edging, always fold crust overhang under slightly beyond the plate's edge and build up rim. The following are "right hand" directions. If you are left handed, use the opposite fingers.

SCALLOPED EDGING - Lay left thumb and index finger flat on outside of rim about 1/2 to 3/4 inch apart. With right index finger pull pastry in toward center of pie and slightly downward. Plan ahead so your spacing will come out even.

PINCHED EDGING - Place left hand fingers in same position as for Scalloped Edging and right index finger pointing directly between them. Pinch

DECORATING TOPS

pastry tightly around right finger. Go over points a second time to sharpen them. Always exaggerate edgings as they will relax and shrink slightly during baking.

FORK EDGING - After folding under overhang, press around edge with fork tines. Dip tines in flour as you go to prevent them from sticking.

COILED EDGING - Place thumb on edge of pie at an angle. Pinch dough between knuckle of index finger and thumb. Press and twist knuckle toward thumb. Repeat at same angle around rim.

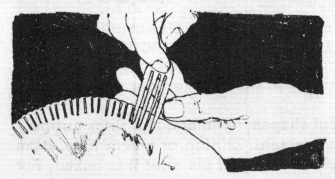

DECORATIVE TOPS

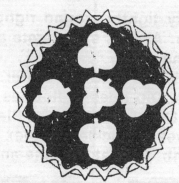

Some pies are traditionally double crusted, but many pies can be "topped" according to the baker's artistic flair. You may want to celebrate a seasonal holiday or special occasion by using decorative pastry cut-outs on top of pie, or you may just be short on dough. Don't let it show, take your tools and be creative.

Using a cookie cutter or free hand, cut shapes, numbers, etc. Prick cut-outs with fork tines. If they are to be used on custard, chiffon or cream pies, bake them separately on a cookie sheet and place on top of pie after it is baked. For

firmer, less juicy pies such as mincemeat, bake the cut-outs on top of filling right along with the pie.

Cut strips of dough in varying widths. Bake separately or on top of pie, depending on consistency of filling. Cut pie with a strip in the center of each piece of pie. This effect gives a finished look but emphasizes the filling. There are fewer calories, too, for those who care.

Cut strips of dough and make decorative designs.

Using a cookie cutter or free hand, cut decorative designs out of top crust before it is placed on filling. Sprinkle sugar on the cut-outs and bake for snacks.

LATTICE TOPS

OLD-FASHIONED LATTICE TOP - Cut top crust in 1/2-inch strips, using a knife for straight edges or a pastry wheel for fancy ones. Moisten rim of bottom crust. Lay half of strips across filling, 1 inch apart. Press ends tightly to rim and brush strips with milk or water so cross strips will stick to them. Lay the remaining strips at right angles to first strips and the same distance apart. Trim strip ends evenly with bottom crust overhang. Bring overhang up over strips. Press firmly around edge to seal. Flute as desired.

WOVEN LATTICE TOP - Cut strips as for Old-Fashioned Lattice Top. Place 5 or 6 across filling. Weave a cross-strip through center by first folding back

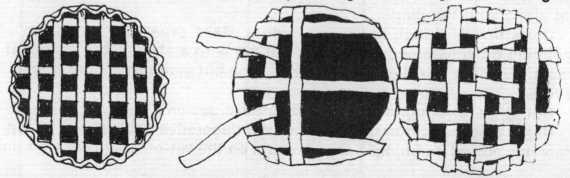

every other strip going the opposite direction. Continue weaving until lattice is complete, folding back alternate strips each time a cross-strip is added. If desired, weave lattice top on a piece of waxed paper and then slip onto pie.

DIAMOND LATTICE TOP - Follow directions for Woven or Old-Fashioned Lattice Tops except place a second set of strips diagonally across first strips.

CURLY TOP LATTICE - Cut thin strips. Twist as tightly as desired (and as much as your dough will withstand), laying them in desired effect on top of filling.

39

Fruit Pies

Pie is claimed to be America's favorite dessert. In fact, apple pie has been a tradition in this country for more than 200 years.

When I was growing up in the Midwest, pie baking, especially in the summer, was a common household occurance. Of all pies, fruit pies were baked most often. From the first strawberries and rhubarb of Spring, to apricots, peaches, blueberries, cherries and the many other succulent offerings of Summer, to the tart apples of Fall, there was a continuous parade of luscious fruits to be baked in flaky crust and served warm with heavy cream, whipped or poured, vanilla ice cream that melted into the fruit, or with delicious sauces which gave the pie a different personality.

Pie may not have originated here, but we have developed and perfected it to its finest point. Our wonderful abundance of fruits has contributed greatly to our pie baking expertise and fondness for this dessert.

I hope you will enjoy the old-fashioned favorites I have included here.

FARM APPLE PIE

Apples for pies should be tart, firm and juicy. Some of the best are Rhode Island Greening, Golden Delicious, Jonathan, McIntosh and Rome Beauty.

Lemon-Egg Crust, page 25   2-crust, unbaked
or Never Fail Crust, page 24

3/4 cup sugar	1/4 tsp. nutmeg	7 cups sliced, peeled apples
2 tbs. flour	1/4 tsp. salt	2 tbs. butter
1 tsp. cinnamon		

42

Line 9-inch pie plate with bottom crust. Roll out top crust. Chill both until needed. Combine sugar, flour, cinnamon, nutmeg and salt. Mix lightly with apples. Heap into prepared pie shell. Dot with butter and add top crust. Finish edges as desired. Bake at 425° F. 50 to 60 minutes. Serve with cheese slices, cinnamon ice cream or with Tangy Mincemeat Sauce, page 85.

VARIATION - Make extra large steam vents. Five minutes before pie is done, pour 1/2 cup heavy cream through slits and bake 5 minutes longer. Serve warm.

AUNT HELEN'S SOUR CREAM APPLE PIE

Lemon-Egg Crust, page 25   1-crust, unbaked
2 tbs. flour   2 cups <u>finely</u> chopped apples
1/8 tsp. salt   1/4 cup sugar
1/2 cup sugar   1/4 cup brown sugar
1 egg, unbeaten   1 tsp. cinnamon
1 cup sour cream   1/4 cup butter
1 tsp. vanilla   1/3 cup flour
1/2 tsp. nutmeg

43

    Line a 9-inch pie plate with crust. Finish edges as desired. Refrigerate until needed. Mix flour, salt and the 1/2 cup sugar. Add egg, sour cream, vanilla and nutmeg. Beat to a smooth batter. Stir in chopped apples. Pour mixture into prepared crust. Bake at 400° F. 15 minutes. Reduce temperature to 350° F. and continue baking 30 to 40 minutes. While pie is baking, combine remaining ingredients for topping. Remove pie from oven and increase temperature to 400° F. Sprinkle topping over pie. Bake 10 minutes longer.

NORTH WOODS BLUEBERRY PIE

Part of any summer visit to my Dad's hometown of International Falls, Minnesota, was spent picking blueberries - for pies, of course!

Mom's Flaky Crust, page 11   2-crust, unbaked
3-1/2 cups fresh blueberries
<u>or</u> 1 pkg. (16 ozs.) unsweetened frozen blueberries
2 tbs. lemon juice
1 tbs. grated lemon rind
3/4 cup sugar
1/4 tsp. salt
2 tbs. flour

44

Line a 9-inch pie plate with crust. Roll out top crust and chill both until needed. Wash and drain blueberries (partially thaw frozen ones). Add lemon juice, rind, sugar, salt and flour. Mix well and fill pie shell. Cover with vented top crust or make a lattice top. Bake 10 minutes at 450° F. Reduce temperature to 350° F. and bake 30 minutes longer. Serve hot or cold.

CINNAMON GLAZED CHERRY PIE

Never-Fail Crust, page 24   1-crust unbaked
4 cups pitted fresh tart cherries
3/4 cup sugar
1/8 tsp. salt
1/4 cup flour
3 tbs. lemon juice
2 tbs. butter
3/4 cup red currant jelly*
1/2 tsp. cinnamon
whipped cream

   Line 9-inch pie plate with crust. Finish edges as desired. Chill until needed. Combine cherries, sugar, salt, flour and lemon juice. Pour into prepared pie shell. Dot with butter. Bake at 375° F. 40 minutes. Cool on rack. Melt jelly over hot water. Blend cinnamon in well. Spoon over cherries. Serve with whipped cream.
*or any tart, red jelly

PEACHY PIE

Delicious served plain or with Cinnamon Blueberry Sauce, page 84.

Mom's Flaky Crust, page 11   2-crust, unbaked
3/4 cup sugar
3 tbs. flour
1/2 tsp. cinnamon or nutmeg
1/8 tsp. salt
5 cups sliced fresh peaches

1 tsp. lemon juice
1/8 tsp. almond extract
2 tbs. butter
1 tbs. sugar

Line a 9-inch pie plate with bottom crust. Roll out top crust. Chill both until needed. Combine sugar, flour, cinnamon and salt. Add to peaches. Stir in lemon juice and almond extract. Pour into prepared pie shell and dot with butter. Cover filling with vented top crust. Finish edges as desired. Sprinkle sugar on top. Bake at 425° F. 40 to 45 minutes, or until peaches are tender and crust is browned.

PEACH-BLUEBERRY PIE - Follow Peachy Pie recipe but slice only 3 cups of peaches. Place 2 cups blueberries in pie shell. Sprinkle with half of dry ingredients and half of lemon juice. Top with peaches. Sprinkle with remaining sugar-flour mixture and lemon juice. Omit almond extract. Dot with butter. Bake as for Peachy Pie.

Hint - Keep peeled peaches in bowl of milk, heavy fruit juice or a solution of ascorbic acid to prevent discoloring. Slice as needed.

HERTHA'S GLAZED PEACH PIE

So fresh tasting it's the next thing to eating just-picked peaches.

Mom's Flaky Crust, page 11   1-crust, baked
8 peaches, peeled
1 cup sugar
1 tbs. cornstarch
1 cup heavy cream, whipped
sugar
1/4 tsp. almond extract, optional

48

Line a 9-inch pie plate with crust. Finish edges as desired. Prick with fork and chill if time allows. Bake as directed. Cool on wire rack until needed. Slice 4 peaches into baked shell. Slice remaining peaches into large saucepan. Combine sugar and cornstarch. Add to peaches and stir to mix. Bring to boil, stirring, and cook until thickened. Pour cooked mixture over raw peaches. Top with lightly sweetened whipped cream, flavored with almond extract. Chill until serving time.

STRAWBERRY GLACE PIE

Select the prettiest berries of similar size to be left whole, and use the misshapen, large or slightly bruised ones for the cooked mixture.

Mom's Flaky Crust, page 11
6 cups (about 1-1/2 quarts)
   strawberries
1 cup sugar
3 tbs. cornstarch

1-crust, baked
1/2 cup water
1 pkg. (3 ozs.) cream cheese, optional
1 to 2 tbs. milk

Line 9-inch pie plate with crust. Finish edges as desired. Prick with fork and chill if time allows. Bake as directed. Cool on wire rack until needed. Wash and hull strawberries. Mash enough berries to measure 1 cup. Blend sugar and cornstarch together in saucepan. Stir in water and crushed berries. Cook, stirring constantly, until mixture thickens and boils. Boil, stirring, 1 minute. Cool. Beat cream cheese with milk. Spread on bottom of baked pie shell. Fill shell with whole berries. Pour cooked mixture over top. Refrigerate several hours. Garnish with whipped cream.

ARLENE'S LEMON PIE

Lemon-Egg Crust, page 25 2-crust, unbaked
3 fresh lemons
2 tbs. finely grated lemon rind
3 eggs
1/3 cup soft butter
1-1/2 cups sugar

1/2 cup water
3 tbs. flour
pinch salt
sugar

Line a 9-inch pie plate with crust. Trim edges. Roll out top crust. Chill both until needed. Grate rind and carefully peel all white membrane from the lemons. Slice as thinly as possible and remove seeds. You should have about 6 ounces of sliced fruit. Beat eggs until foamy. Set aside. Using same beaters, cream butter and sugar. Continue beating at low speed, adding water, flour and salt. Stir in lemon slices and beaten eggs. Fold in lemon rind. Pour mixture into prepared shell. Cover with vented top crust. Finish edges as desired. Sprinkle liberally with sugar. Bake at 450° F. and bake 45 minutes longer. Cool before slicing.

RHUBARB CUSTARD PIE

Aunt Katy would send plenty of these special springtime pies out to the thrashers for an afternoon snack with tall jars of chilled coffee. A jar of thick cream would go along for both pie and coffee.

Lemon-Egg Crust, page 25   2-crust, unbaked
or Never-Fail Crust, page 24

1 cup sugar	1 tbs. butter, softened	3 cups (1 in. pieces) rhubarb
3 tbs. flour	2 eggs	powdered sugar
1/2 tsp. nutmeg		

Line a 9-inch pie plate with crust. Brush shell with egg white. Roll out top crust. Chill both until needed. Combine sugar, flour, nutmeg, butter and eggs. Beat until smooth. Place rhubarb in pie shell. Pour egg mixture over rhubarb. Cover with top crust or lattice topping. Finish edges as desired. Bake at 450° F. 10 minutes. Reduce temperature to 350° F. and bake 30 minutes longer. Sprinkle pie with sugar when it come out of the oven. Delicious served warm with heavy cream poured over or with Spicy Sour Cream Sauce, page 85.

SOUR CREAM RAISIN PIE

This is without a doubt my Dad's favorite pie. While it was baking Mom would "cook coffee" as we say in Minnesota. It's a special egg coffee (see page 84 in "Cakes") that is so clear you won't believe it's strong.

Lemon-Egg Crust, page 25   1-crust, unbaked
3 egg yolks, slightly beaten   3/4 tsp. cinnamon
1 cup sour cream   1/4 tsp. cloves
1 cup firmly-packed brown sugar   1/4 tsp. salt
1 cup chopped seedless raisins

52

Line 9-inch pie plate with crust. Finish edges as desired and brush shell with egg white. Chill. Combine egg yolks, sour cream, sugar, raisins, spices and salt. Pour into unbaked pie shell. Bake 10 minutes at 450° F. Reduce temperature to 350° F. and bake 30 minutes longer. Serve cold with whipped cream, ice cream or make a meringue as directed on page 82. Add 1/4 cup chopped nuts to meringue mixture. Spread over hot pie, being careful to seal to the edge of crust. Bake 15 minutes at 325° F. until meringue is lightly browned.

FESTIVE MINCE PIE

Never-Fail Crust, page 24   1-crust, unbaked
3 cups (28 oz. jar) mincemeat
1-1/2 cups chopped apple
3 tbs. brandy

Line a 9-inch pie plate with crust. Finish edges as desired. Chill until needed. Mix mincemeat, apple and brandy well. Pour into prepared pie shell. Bake at 425° F. for 40 to 45 minutes. Mince pie can also be baked with a top crust, a lattice top or with pastry cut-outs (see page 36). For a delicious treat, serve hot Old Fashioned Lemon Sauce, page 84, with the double crusted pie.

VARIATION - Pour a tablespoon or two of brandy or half brandy and half sherry through vents in a double-crust pie when it is completely baked. Serve with cheese.

DEEP DISH PLUM PIE

If you like more filling and less crust, deep dish pies are perfect. They are quick to make and can be baked in almost any round, square or oblong casserole-type dish.

Mom's Flaky Crust, page 11   1-crust, unbaked
or Never-Fail Crust, page 24

54

5 cups (about 2 lbs.) purple plums
3/4 cup firmly-packed brown sugar
2 tsp. quick-cooking tapioca
1/4 tsp. cinnamon

dash of salt
dash of nutmeg
1 tbs. butter

Prepare crust. Roll dough slightly larger than dish. Cut to fit dish allowing for overhang. Cut vents and chill until needed. Pit and halve plums. Combine plums, sugar, tapioca, cinnamon, salt and nutmeg. Let stand 15 minutes. Place in baking dish. Dot with butter. Place vented crust over filling. Fold edges under, anchor to rim of dish and flute. Bake at 375° F. 40 to 45 minutes. Serve warm with cream or ice cream.

DEEP DISH VARIATIONS

Follow the directions for Deep-Dish Plum pie, using any of the following fillings.

DEEP DISH CHERRY - 8 cups pitted, tart, fresh cherries, 2-2/3 cups sugar, 1/8 teaspoon salt, 2/3 cup flour and 3 tablespoons butter.

DEEP DISH PEACH or APRICOT - 8 cups peeled and sliced fresh, firm peaches or unpeeled apricots, 2 cups sugar, 1/8 teaspoon salt, 1/2 cup flour, 1/2 teaspoon cinnamon and 3 tablespoons butter.

DEEP DISH APPLE - 8 cups sliced, peeled apples, 1 cup sugar, 1/4 cup flour, 1/2 teaspoon cinnamon, 1/8 teaspoon nutmeg, 1/8 teaspoon salt, 1 tablespoon lemon juice and 2 tablespoons butter.

Custard-Type Pies

The ideal egg-custard pie has a firm filling, a crusty shell and a subtle flavor hinting of vanilla, nutmeg or lemon.

Custard pies have a reputation for being "tricky" to make. Little wonder since high heat is necessary for a good crust, but low heat is needed for the custard which is thickened by eggs only. A fair solution is two-temperature baking. Custard pies are usually started in a hot 450° F. oven for 20 minutes to set the crust, then finished at 350° F., which is a more suitable temperature for the custard.

A technique which many consider an answer to the dilemma is to bake the crust and filling separately and combine them by what is known as the slip-slide method (see page 59). It may take a little practice at first but it's worth the try.

If you're not ready for the "slip-slide", brushing the unbaked pie shell with egg white and dusting with nutmeg helps considerably to prevent a soggy bottom crust. And so does cooling the baked pie on a rack to allow air to circulate underneath and keep it from steaming.

Custard pies should be eaten within 3 hours, otherwise they must be refrigerated and chilling causes them to "weep" and become soggy.

VELVETY CUSTARD PIE

Never-Fail Crust, page 24   1-crust, unbaked
or Mom's Flaky Crust, page 11
4 eggs
2/3 cup sugar
1/2 tsp. salt
1/4 tsp. nutmeg
2-2/3 cups milk
1 tsp. vanilla

58

Line a 9-inch pie plate with crust. Build rim as high as possible to accommodate the custard filling. Finish edges as desired. Brush bottom with egg white and sprinkle lightly with nutmeg. Chill until needed. Preheat oven to 450° F. Beat eggs slightly with mixer. Beat in sugar, salt, nutmeg, milk and vanilla on medium speed. To prevent having to move pie after it is filled, pull oven rack partially out of oven. Place empty pie shell in center of rack. Pour filling into shell and carefully slide rack back into oven. Bake pie at 450° F. 20 minutes. Reduce temperature to 350° F. and bake 20 minutes longer, or until

knife inserted near the center of the pie comes clean and center is still slightly soft. Do not bake until center is set as the pie will continue to bake after it is removed from the oven. Overbaking causes "weeping" and a soggy crust. Serve slightly warm or at room temperature. Do not refrigerate.

SLIP-SLIDE CUSTARD PIE - Preheat oven to 350° F. Prepare filling as for Velvety Custard Pie, but instead pour mixture into an <u>ungreased pie plate</u>. Place in shallow pan of hot water. Bake about 65 minutes or until knife inserted near center comes out clean. Remove from oven and cool to lukewarm. Bake crust while filling cools. When both are cool, loosen custard around edge of plate with spatula. Shake gently to loosen completely and slip custard into baked shell. Let settle a few minutes before serving. If the filling cracks or breaks, slip it in anyway. Remedy by smoothing whipped cream over surface. No one will know, and the taste will be surperb!

PUMPKIN PIE

For holiday dinners Mom always baked our favorite, Pumpkin Pie, and a Have 'Em Both Pie for those who wanted pumpkin <u>and</u> mince.

Lemon-Egg Crust, page 25   1-crust, unbaked
1-1/4 cups cooked or canned pumpkin
3/4 cup sugar
1/2 tsp. salt
1/2 tsp. ginger
1 tsp. cinnamon
1 tsp. flour
2 eggs, slightly beaten
1 cup evaporated milk
2 tbs. water
1/2 tsp. vanilla

Line a 9-inch pie plate with crust. Build rim as high as possible to accommodate filling. Finish edges as desired. Brush bottom of crust with egg

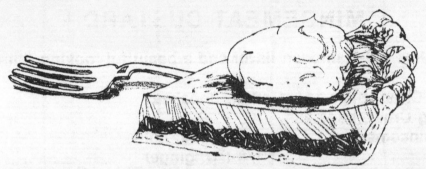

white. Chill until needed. Combine pumpkin, sugar, salt, spices and flour in mixing bowl. Add eggs and mix well. Stir in evaporated milk, water and vanilla. To avoid having to move the pie after it is filled, pull oven rack partially out of oven. Place empty pie shell in center of rack. Pour filling into shell and carefully slide rack back into oven. Bake at 400° F. 45 to 50 minutes, or until knife inserted half way between edge and center comes out clean. Serve cool, not chilled, with whipped cream, ice cream or Tangy Mincemeat Sauce, page 85.

HAVE 'EM BOTH PIE - Reduce pumpkin to 1 cup and spread 3/4 cup mincemeat on bottom crust. Pour pumpkin mixture over mincemeat. Bake as directed. Serve warm with whipped cream or ice cream.

MINCEMEAT CUSTARD

This pie has old-fashioned flavor and a beautiful-looking filling.

Mom's Flaky Crust, page 11   1-crust, unbaked
or Lemon-Egg Crust, page 25

1-3/4 cups mincemeat   1 cup milk, cold
2 tbs. flour   1/8 tsp. ginger
3/4 cup brown sugar   3 tbs. lemon juice
1/8 tsp. salt   2 tbs. finely-grated lemon rind
3 tbs. butter   2 egg whites, stiffly beaten
2 egg yolks, slightly beaten

Line a 9-inch pie plate with crust. Finish edges as desired. Chill until needed. Spread mincemeat in pie shell. In mixer bowl combine flour, brown sugar and salt. With mixer on medium speed blend in butter. Add egg yolks, milk, ginger, lemon juice and rind and beat until smooth. Fold in stiffly beaten egg whites. Pour mixture over mincemeat. Bake 10 minutes at 450° F. Reduce temperature to 325° F. and bake 45 minutes longer. Serve warm or cold.

AUNT AGNES' PECAN PIE

There certainly are no secrets to this recipe, but somehow my aunt's pies always tasted better than any other pecan pies. If you want more filling, increase the recipe by a third.

Mom's Flaky Crust, page 11
or Never-Fail Crust, page 24
3 eggs
1 cup dark corn syrup
1/4 cup sugar

1-crust, unbaked

3 tbs. melted butter
1 tsp. vanilla
1 cup pecans, coarsely chopped

Line a 9-inch pie plate with crust and finish edges as desired. Brush shell with egg white and do not prick. Chill until needed. Combine eggs, corn syrup, sugar, butter and vanilla in bowl. Beat until well blended. Stir in pecans. Pour mixture into prepared pie shell. Bake at 350° F. 35 to 45 minutes, until knife inserted near center comes out clean. For an extra delicious treat, serve topped with whipped cream.

Cream Pies

Many pies fit in the category of cream pies. Basically the cream pie filling is a combination of milk, eggs, flour or cornstarch, sugar and flavoring. Cooking takes place in a double boiler over hot water, or in a heavy saucepan over medium heat. Stirring must be constant to prevent lumpIng. Smoothness is essential in a good cream pie.

It is wise to beat the eggs before adding to the milk mIxture. Do not overthicken. Test by making a path through the middle of mIxture with your wooden spoon. It should part but come together again slowly. Remove mixture from heat and press plastic wrap directly onto surface to prevent it from drying on top and forming a crust. Refrigerate. When chilled, stir thoroughly, add flavoring, and pour into baked shell. Press plastic wrap over filling if there is no whipped cream or meringue topping.

VANILLA CREAM PIE

Use this basic recipe for other cream pies including the all-time favorite - banana cream. Experiment with variety and cookie crusts.

Mom's Flaky Crust, page 11 1-crust, baked
2/3 cup sugar   4 egg yolks, slightly beaten
1/4 cup cornstarch   2 tbs. butter, softened
1/2 tsp. salt   1 tbs. plus 1 tsp. vanilla
3 cups milk   sweetened whipped cream

Line a 9-inch pie plate with crust. Finish edges as desired. Prick shell with a fork. Chill if time allows. Bake as directed. Cool on rack until needed. In saucepan blend sugar, cornstarch and salt. Blend milk into egg yolks. Stir egg mixture slowly into dry ingredients. Cook, stirring constantly, over medium heat until mixture thickens and boils. (Use a wooden spoon, preferably one with a flat edge and scrape sides and bottom of pan constantly. You want to avoid even the slightest hint of burnt or browned cream.) Boil, stirring, 1 minute. Remove from heat and blend in butter and vanilla. Immediately pour into baked pie shell.

Press plastic wrap <u>directly onto filling</u> (this will prevent a crust from forming). Chill pie 2 hours or longer. Just before serving, remove plastic wrap and top with sweetened whipped cream.

CHOCOLATE CREAM PIE - Follow recipe for Vanilla Cream Pie except increase sugar to 1-1/4 cups and cornstarch to 1/3 cup. Cut up 2 squares (1 ounce each) unsweetened chocolate and add with milk. Omit butter. You may wish to decrease vanilla to your taste, or substitute rum or brandy flavoring.

BUTTERSCOTCH CREAM PIE - Follow the recipe for Vanilla Cream Pie except substitute 1 cup brown sugar for granulated sugar and decrease vanilla to 1 teaspoon.

BANANA CREAM PIE - Follow Vanilla Cream Pie recipe. Press plastic wrap onto filling in <u>saucepan and cool to room temperature</u>. Slice 2 large bananas into baked pie shell in layers and pour cooled filling on top.

COCONUT CREAM PIE - Follow Vanilla Cream Pie recipe except decrease vanilla to 2 teaspoons and stir in 1 cup flaked coconut. Sprinkle additional coconut (toasted, if you like) over whipped cream topping.

SKY HIGH LEMON PIE

Lemon-Egg Crust, page 25   1-crust, baked
or Mom's Flaky Crust, page 11, or Never-Fail Crust, page 24

1-1/2 tbs. butter	5 egg yolks, beaten
3/4 cup sugar	grated rind and juice of 1 lemon
3 tbs. flour	1 cup hot water plus 1/2 cup lemon juice

68   Line a 9-inch pie plate with crust. Finish edges as desired. Prick shell with fork and chill if time allows. Bake as directed. Cool on rack until needed. Melt butter in top of double boiler over hot water. Mix sugar and flour in a bowl. Add beaten yolks, lemon rind and juice. Slowly stir in hot water-juice mixture. Add mixture to butter. Cook until thick, stirring constantly. Cool thoroughly with plastic wrap pressed against filling. Stir well to assure smooth texture and pour into baked shell. Cover immediately with meringue* and bake. Cool and serve as soon as possible. Meringue pies do not hold up well.

*See detailed directions for making meringue on page 82. Because this is a special pie, I use at least 5 egg whites and sometimes more.

ANGEL PIES

Prepare and bake a Meringue Pie Shell as directed on page 30. Be sure to build the meringue up into a high rim, especially for the Lemon Custard version which has several layers.

CHOCOLATE ANGEL PIE - Melt 3/4 cup semisweet chocolate pieces in double boiler over hot water. Remove from heat and slowly stir in 1/4 cup hot water. Add 1 teaspoon vanilla and 1/8 teaspoon salt. Stir gently until blended. Pour into mixing bowl and cool. Whip 1 cup heavy cream and fold into cooled chocolate. Fill prepared shell. Chill at least 4 hours or all day if possible. Serve topped with whipped cream.

LEMON CUSTARD ANGEL PIE - Combine 3/4 cup sugar, 7 tablespoons cornstarch and 1/4 teaspoon salt. Stir in 2-1/2 cups milk. Cook, stirring, over medium heat until thickened. Beat 6 egg yolks until light. Blend milk mixture into eggs. Return to saucepan and cook, stirring, until thickened. Remove from heat. Stir in 1/2 cup lemon juice and 3 tablespoons finely-grated lemon peel. Chill. Whip 1 cup heavy cream until stiff. Spread alternate layers of cold lemon filling and cream in meringue shell, starting and ending with lemon filling. Chill at least 4 hours, or all day.

Chiffon Pies

Good chiffon pies are light and airy with no trace of gelatin bits in the filling. Correct treatment of the gelatin and egg whites and use of the proper method of combining the two will give you the best pie.

GELATIN TIPS

Always use cold liquid (water or fruit juice) to soften unflavored gelatin, and sprinkle the gelatin <u>on top</u> of liquid.

Add softened gelatin to hot liquid and sugar and stir until gelatin is dissolved.

Gelatin mixture thickens faster when chilled in a shallow dish. If refrigerator space is not available set pan with gelatin mixture in a pan of ice water. Stir occasionally.

Chill until mixture mounds slightly when dropped from spoon. It should be slightly thicker than unbeaten egg whites. The secret is not to let it get firm. Have egg whites ready, because the gelatin mixture will continue to thicken at room temperature.

If mixture does become too thick, set over warm water and melt. Chill again, watching very closely, and continue as before.

EGG WHITE TIPS

Egg whites separate from yolks best when cold, but beat to better volume when at room temperature.

Wash beaters in hot soapy water before using for egg whites.

Beat egg whites on medium-low speed until frothy. Add cream of tartar and beat on highest speed until stiff, but not dry.

COMBINING AND FINISHING TIPS

Gently fold several spoonfuls of whites into gelatin mixture.

Then fold gelatin mixture into whites in 3 stages. Using a slotted spoon, fold down the side of the bowl, across the bottom, up over the other side, and over the top again, occasionally cutting through the middle. <u>Never stir or beat egg whites into gelatin mixture.</u>

Test for mounding when whites are incorporated. If the mixture is too soft, chill it until it will mound. Then turn into a pie shell and swirl top. Refrigerate immediately. If pie is to be frozen, place in freezer unwrapped. When frozen solid, place in freezer bag. Before serving, defrost in refrigerator 1-1/2 hours. Add whipped cream topping just before serving.

RASPBERRY FLUFF PIE

In the middle of winter this pie tasted of spring and in the summer with fresh berries it was a cool breeze to refresh us.

Mom's Flaky Crust, page 11   1-crust, baked
1 pkg. (12 ozs.) frozen raspberries   1 cup heavy cream
1 tbs. gelatin   2 tbs. powdered sugar
1 cup raspberry juice

Line a 9-inch pie plate with crust and finish edges as desired. Prick shell and chill if time allows. Bake as directed. Cool on rack until needed. Thaw berries and drain well. Save juice. Add water if necessary to make 1 cup. Measure 1/4 cup juice into mixing bowl. Sprinkle gelatin over juice and set aside to soften. Heat the remaining 3/4 cup juice and pour over softened gelatin. Stir until gelatin is dissolved. Chill until almost set. Beat until very fluffy. Fold in raspberries. Whip cream and sugar together until stiff. Fold into whipped gelatin. Pour into baked shell and chill or freeze. Garnish with whipped cream and chopped, salted nuts, if desired.

KEY LIME PIE

Lemon-Egg Crust, page 25   1-crust, baked
or Never-Fail Crust, page 24
1 tbs. gelatin   1/4 tsp. salt
1/4 cup cold water   grated rind of 1 lime
4 eggs, separated   1 cup whipping cream
1 cup sugar   2 tbs. powdered sugar
1/2 cup lime juice

74

Line a 9-inch pie plate with crust. Finish edges as desired. Prick shell with fork and chill if time allows. Bake as directed and cool on rack until needed. Sprinkle gelatin over cold water. Beat egg yolks in the top of double boiler. Add 1/2 cup sugar, lime juice and salt. Place over hot water and cook, stirring constantly, until the custard coats the spoon. Add softened gelatin and cook a few minutes longer until gelatin is dissolved. Remove from heat and add rind. Cool. Beat egg whites until frothy. Add remaining 1/2 cup sugar, a spoonful at a time, and beat until stiff. Fold into custard. Pour into shell and chill. At serving time whip cream with sugar and spread over pie.

RUM CHIFFON PIE

Graham Cracker Crust #1, page 27   1-crust, baked
1 tbs. gelatin   3/4 cup sugar   3 tbs. rum *
1/4 cup cold water   1/8 tsp. salt   1/2 cup heavy cream, whipped
1-1/2 cups milk   3 eggs, separated

Prepare pie crust as directed. Bake and cool on rack until needed. Soften
gelatin in cold water. Scald milk in double boiler. Add sugar and salt and stir
until sugar is dissolved. Gradually add well-beaten egg yolks, beating
constantly. Cook over hot water, stirring constantly until custard thickens
slightly and coats the back of spoon. Add gelatin and stir until dissolved. Cool
until mixture starts to set. Stir in rum. Beat egg whites until stiff, but not dry.
Fold into custard. Mound into pie shell and chill thoroughly. When ready to
serve, top with whipped cream. Serve very cold.

*try brandy or apple brandy

BITTERSWEET CHOCOLATE MINT PIE

You'll have a stack of pans to wash - but it's worth it.

Lemon-Egg Crust, page 25   1-crust, baked
<u>or</u> Never-Fail Crust, page 24
1/2 cup sugar
1 env. (1 tbs.) unflavored gelatin
1 tbs. cornstarch
1 cup milk
3 eggs, separated
1 sq. (1 oz.) unsweetened chocolate, melted and cooled
1/2 cup heavy cream
1/3 cup green creme de menthe

Line a 9-inch pie plate with crust. Finish edges as desired. Prick shell with a fork and chill if time allows. Bake as directed and cool on rack until needed. In saucepan combine 1/4 cup sugar, gelatin and cornstarch. Stir in milk. Cook, stirring, over medium heat until gelatin is dissolved. Stir about half of hot

mixture into slightly beaten egg yolks. Return to saucepan mixture. Cook and stir 2 minutes longer. Divide mixture in half. Stir chocolate into one half and chill until partially set. Leave remaining half of mixture at room temperature. Beat egg whites to soft peaks. Gradually add remaining 1/4 cup sugar and continue beating until stiff peaks form. Whip cream and fold into meringue. Stir half of meringue mixture (chill the remaining half) into chocolate mixture. Pour into baked pie shell and chill 30 minutes. Stir creme de menthe into remaining gelatin mixture and chill until partially set. Fold in remaining meringue mixture Spoon over chocolate layer. Chill several hours or overnight. Garnish with additional whipped cream and shaved chocolate.

Toppings, Sauces & End Alls

Next to a la mode the two favorite pie toppings are whipped cream and fluffy, lightly browned meringue. Sauces, too can completely change a pie.

WHIPPING CREAM

Whipping is more than just "beating" the cream. Heavy cream (40% butterfat) is the best for whipping. With the incorportion of air it will expand from 1 cup to 2. For best results try these suggestions.

Have heavy cream very cold and chill bowl and beaters.

Begin beating slowly with mixer on low speed until cream begins to foam. Increase speed gradually to moderate until cream holds soft peaks. Avoid beating too much. Do not go beyond the smooth stage or you might end up with butter!

Use a rubber spatula to scrape down the sides of bowl once or twice during beating.

Add powdered or super-fine sugar gradually, using 2 to 4 tablespoons per cup of cream.

Add flavoring (vanilla, liquor, etc.) just before serving.

If an extra fluffy topping is desired, combine equal parts of whipped cream and stiffly beaten egg whites.

Cream that is reluctant will whip more quickly if you add a few drops of lemon juice.

VARIATIONS

Use 2 tablespoons honey in place of sugar.
Fold 2 tablespoons finely grated lemon or orange rind into whipped cream.
Fold 1/2 cup chopped nuts into whipped cream.
Add a dash of cinnamon.
Add 1 square (1 ounce) melted bittersweet chocolate and 3 tablespoons
sugar to 1/2 cup cream before whipping.

MERINGUE

Meringue should not be limited to lemon pies. Pies of all kinds are enhanced by the addition of a pretty billowy topping. Here are a few basic suggestions which are helpful in making perfect meringues every time.

Have egg whites at room temperature, and the beaters and bowl absolutely free of any grease. Wash in hot soapy water and rinse well to be sure.

Add 1 teaspoon water per egg to increase volume.

Add 1/4 teaspoon cream of tartar per egg white for added stiffness.

Use 2 tablespoons super-fine or powdered sugar per egg white. Too much sugar gives a gummy crust with sugar crystals, while too little sugar gives a less fluffy, less tender meringue.

Beat egg whites until frothy, add cream of tartar and beat until stiff, but not dry. On high speed beat in sugar a very small amount at a time. Add flavoring and beat until whites stand in stiff peaks. Do not overbeat.

Immediately swirl meringue over pie. Build up high for a pretty effect - do

82

not smooth top. Be sure meringue is attached to crust well or it will shrink away from sides while baking.

Bake in preheated 350° F. oven 12 to 15 minutes.

Cool at room temperature away from drafts.

VARIATIONS

Instead of vanilla use 1/2 teaspoon almond extract or 2 teaspoons instant coffee powder or 2 teaspoons brandy or Kirsch. Add a few drops of lemon juice with each.

Use 1/3 cup honey and a little lemon juice. Add very slowly 1 teaspoon at a time while beating.

Fold in 1/2 cup cocoa or 1/4 cup grated bitter chocolate or salted chopped nuts or lemon rind.

Sprinkle 1/4 cup shredded, long-grain coconut over meringue before placing in oven.

OLD-FASHIONED LEMON SAUCE

3/4 cup sugar   1/4 cup water   1/4 tsp. grated lemon rind
1/2 cup butter   1 egg, well beaten   3 tbs. lemon juice

Combine all ingredients in saucepan. Heat to boiling over medium heat, stirring constantly. Serve warm or cool. Store in covered container in refrigerator.

84

CINNAMON BLUEBERRY SAUCE

1 cup fresh or frozen blueberries   1 tbs. lemon juice
2 tbs. water   1 tsp. cornstarch
2 tbs. sugar   1/4 tsp. cinnamon

Combine all ingredients in saucepan. Heat to boiling over medium heat, stirring constantly. Reduce heat and simmer 5 minutes, stirring occasionally. Serve warm or cool.

SPICY SOUR CREAM TOPPING

1 cup sour cream   1/2 tsp. cinnamon
2 tbs. sugar   1/8 tsp. nutmeg

Blend ingredients. Spread on top of fruit pies for a different touch. Substitute lemon or orange peel or vanilla for spices.

CRUNCHY PECAN TOPPING

1/4 cup brown sugar   1/3 cup chopped pecans   2 tbs. light cream

Combine ingredients in small saucepan. Cook over low heat, stirring constantly, until slightly thickened. Spread over <u>warm</u> pie.

TANGY MINCEMEAT SAUCE - Heat 1 cup mincemeat and 1/2 cup port wine or cranberry juice together. Serve warm or store in covered container in refrigerator.

END ALLS

Scraps of dough any size make good snacks for the family. We always called them "eccles", but I don't know why. You may break the never-reroll rule for these. Roll dough and cut into strips 1/2-inch wide or use scraps as they are. Sprinkle with cinnamon-sugar and bake at 450° F. 10 minutes or until browned.

CHEESE STRAWS - These make excellent cocktail snacks. In fact, don't always rely on scraps, but make crust especially for them sometime. Roll pastry to 1/4-inch thickness and cut into 1/4-inch strips. Sprinkle with grated cheese and dust lightly with cayenne. Bake at 450° F. 10 minutes.

CINNAMON STICKS - Roll dough to 1/8-inch thickness. Spread with soft butter. Sprinkle with sugar and cinnamon. Cut into 1 x 4-inch sticks or other shapes. Bake 10 minutes or until brown at 450° F.

JAM TARTS - Cut dough into 3-inch squares. Put 1 to 2 teaspoons jam on each square. Wet edges with cold water and fold over to form a triangle. Press edges together with a fork. Prick top several times. Bake at 425° F. 10 to 12 minutes.

Index

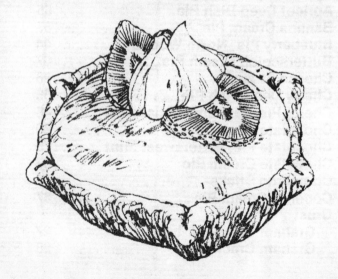